©2024, Frank Young

Table of Contents

For Couples in Relationship:
Personality Compatibilities and Differences
Based on the Chinese Zodiac of Twelve Representing Animals

Frank Young

Poplar House Press, 2024

Foreword

Welcome to a captivating journey into the intricate tapestry of love, compatibility, and self-discovery. In the realm of relationships, where two unique souls intertwine, understanding the nuances of personality becomes an essential compass for navigating the seas of love. In this guide, we delve into the ancient wisdom of the Chinese zodiac, unlocking the secrets it holds for couples seeking harmony and connection.

"For Couples in Relationship: Personality Compatibilities and Differences" (here the word "difference" is sometimes understood to mean "conflict" and "challenge" too) is more than a book; it is a celestial roadmap to understanding the dynamics between partners through the lens of the twelve Chinese zodiac animal representations. As we embark on this exploration, prepare to be enchanted by the rich symbolism and profound insights that each animal brings to the table.

From the spirited Rat to the wise and patient Ox, the dynamic Tiger to the charming Rabbit, every animal in the Chinese zodiac contributes a unique essence to the cosmic dance of relationships. This guide serves as your trusted companion, offering practical advice and profound revelations to enhance your understanding of self and your beloved.

As we navigate the labyrinth of love, remember that differences are not obstacles but opportunities for growth and deeper connection. Embrace the wisdom of the Chinese zodiac as a tool for self-awareness and a roadmap for cultivating enduring love.

May this book be a beacon of light on your journey, illuminating the path towards a harmonious and fulfilling partnership. May you discover the magic that lies within the union of kindred spirits, guided by the timeless wisdom of the Chinese zodiac.

Wishing you a transformative and enriching experience as you explore the enchanting world of personality compatibilities and differences in relationships.

With love and celestial blessings,
Frank Young
West Windsor, New Jersey
February, 2024

The Zodiac Animals of the Chinese Calendar

The twelve representing animals are Rat, Ox, Tiger, Rabbit, Dragon, Snake, Horse, Goat, Monkey, Rooster, Dog, and Pig. We will follow this traditional order in our presentation.

For example, the couples Rabbit-Horse and Horse-Rabbit are both shown as Rabbit-Horse because in the zodiac sign listing Rabbit is placed before Horse.

Here are the zodiac animals by the years of birth by the Chinese calendar.

Rat

1924, 1936, 1948, 1960, 1972, 1984, 1996, 2008, 2020, 2032

Notable people: William Shakespeare, English playwright and poet; George Washington, first president of the United States; Wolfgang Amadeus Mozart, Austrian composer

Ox

1925, 1937, 1949, 1961, 1973, 1985, 1997, 2009, 2021, 2033

Notable people: Vincent van Gogh, Dutch painter; Richard Nixon, 37th President of the United States; Barack Obama, 44th President of the United States

Tiger

1926, 1938, 1950, 1962, 1974, 1986, 1998, 2010, 2022, 2034

Notable people: Marco Polo, Venetian explorer and merchant; Queen Elizabeth II, Queen of the United Kingdom; Marilyn Monroe, American actress

Rabbit

1927, 1939, 1951, 1963, 1975, 1987, 1999, 2011, 2023, 2035

Notable people: Albert Einstein, theoretical physicist; Tina Fey, American actress

Dragon

1928, 1940, 1952, 1964, 1976, 1988, 2000, 2012, 2024, 2036

Notable people: Martin Luther King Jr., civil rights activist; Bruce Lee, American actor

Snake

1929, 1941, 1953, 1965, 1977, 1989, 2001, 2013, 2025, 2037

Notable people: Abraham Lincoln, 16th President of the United States, Pablo Picasso, Spanish painter and sculptor

Horse

1930, 1942, 1954, 1966, 1978, 1990, 2002, 2014, 2026, 2038

Notable people: Nelson Mandela, former president of South Africa and anti-apartheid revolutionary; Joe Biden, 46th president of the United States; Angela Merkel, chancellor of Germany; Jackie Chan, Hong Kong actor

Goat

1931, 1943, 1955, 1967, 1979, 1991, 2003, 2015, 2027, 2039

Notable people: Mark Twain (Samuel Clemens), American author; Bill Gates, co-founder of Microsoft, Steve Jobs, co-founder of Apple

Monkey

1932, 1944, 1956, 1968, 1980, 1992, 2004, 2016, 2028, 2040

Notable people: Leonardo da Vinci, Italian polymath, painter, and inventor; Julius Caesar, Roman general and statesman; Elizabeth Taylor, British actress

Rooster

1933, 1945, 1957, 1969, 1981, 1993, 2005, 2017, 2029, 2041

Notable people: Roger Federer, Swiss professional tennis player; Britney Spears, American singer and actress; Serena Williams, American professional tennis player

Dog

1934, 1946, 1958, 1970, 1982, 1994, 2006, 2018, 2030, 2042

Notable people: Winston Churchill, former prime minister of the United Kingdom; Donald Trump, 45th President of the United States; Steven Spielberg, American filmmaker; Mother Teresa, Albanian-Indian Roman Catholic nun and missionary

Pig

1935, 1947, 1959, 1971, 1983, 1995, 2007, 2019, 2031, 2043

Notable people: Ronald Reagan, 40th President of the United States; Alfred Hitchcock, British film director and producer; Elon Musk, CEO of SpaceX and Tesla

One should also note that the Chinese zodiac signs follow the lunar calendar, which is a lunisolar calendar, rather than the Gregorian calendar, which is a solar calendar.

The Gregorian calendar starts the year on January 1st and each year has 12 months. The Chinese calendar, on the other hand, starts on a new moon and usually falls between January 21st and February 20th of the Gregorian calendar.

Thus, the Chinese New Year often comes with a delay of 20 to 40 days and it may be subtle to determine the zodiac animal sign for someone born in January to early February. For example, 2023 is the Year of Rabbit and 2024 the Year of Dragon. If one was born on January 30th, 2024, one's Chinese calendar birth year is actually 2023 instead of 2024, so that one's animal sign is Rabbit but not Dragon, since January 1st, 2024 in the Chinese calendar is February 10th, 2024, in Gregorian calendar.

Thus, we start our presentation from the couple of Rat and Rat, followed by the couple of Rat and Ox, the couple of Rat and Tiger, and so on.

Rat and Rat

Personality Compatibilities

Shared Values: Rats are generally known for being intelligent, resourceful, and adaptable. When both partners have similar values and outlooks on life, it can create a strong foundation for their relationship.

Communication: Rats are usually articulate and expressive individuals. This shared trait can contribute to effective communication within the relationship, allowing the couple to express their thoughts and feelings openly.

Financial Savvy: Rats are often associated with financial acumen and resourcefulness. When both partners possess these qualities, it can lead to effective financial planning and decision-making, contributing to the overall stability of the marriage.

Intellectual Compatibility: Rats tend to be intellectually curious and quick-witted. When both partners share similar intellectual interests, it can lead to engaging conversations and a mentally stimulating relationship.

Personality Differences

Competitiveness: Rats can be quite competitive, and if not managed well, this trait may lead to conflicts within the relationship. It's important for both partners to recognize each other's strengths and support rather than compete against each other.

Independence: While Rats value their independence, too much independence within the relationship may lead to moments of emotional distance. Balancing independence with togetherness is crucial for a healthy and fulfilling partnership.

Decision-Making Styles: Rats may have strong opinions and preferences, and if both partners are assertive in decision-making, it could lead to power struggles. Finding a balance and learning to compromise will be essential for a harmonious marriage.

Emotional Expression: Rats, while intelligent, may not always be overtly emotional. It's important for the couple to understand and respect each other's emotional needs, ensuring that both partners feel heard and supported.

In essence, a Rat-Rat relationship is characterized by intellectual synergy, resourcefulness, and social compatibility. While they may face challenges related to competitiveness and restlessness, navigating these differences with open communication and mutual understanding can lead to a fulfilling and intellectually stimulating connection. With their combined energy and strategic thinking, the Rat and Rat can embark on a journey of love and growth together.

Rat and Ox

Personality Compatibilities

Complementary Strengths: Rats are known for their intelligence, resourcefulness, and adaptability, while Oxen are characterized by their diligence, reliability, and strong work ethic. The combination of these traits can create a well-balanced partnership where the Rat's creativity is complemented by the Ox's stability and perseverance.

Financial Harmony: Both Rats and Oxen are generally prudent with money. This shared value in financial matters can contribute to effective budgeting, planning, and long-term financial stability for the couple.

Shared Goals: When Rats and Oxen align on common goals and values, they can work together with determination to achieve success. Both signs appreciate security and can contribute to building a stable and comfortable life for themselves and their family.

Respect for Boundaries: Oxen appreciate structure and routine, while Rats value their independence. With mutual respect for each other's need for personal space and autonomy, they can strike a balance that allows for both stability and freedom within the relationship.

Personality Differences

Communication Styles: Rats are generally quick-witted and expressive, while Oxen may be more reserved and practical in their communication. It's important for the couple to understand and adapt to each other's communication styles to avoid misunderstandings.

Approach to Challenges: Rats may prefer taking risks and exploring new ideas, while Oxen tend to be more cautious and methodical. Balancing these different approaches can lead to a well-rounded decision-making process that combines innovation with practicality.

Handling Stress: In times of stress, Rats may be more adaptable and quicker to find solutions, while Oxen may rely on their endurance and perseverance. Understanding and appreciating each other's coping mechanisms can help the couple navigate challenges more effectively.

Social Preferences: Rats are generally social and enjoy networking, while Oxen may be more selective in their social interactions. Finding a balance between socializing and quiet moments is essential for a harmonious relationship.

In summary, a Rat-Ox couple can form a strong and harmonious union by leveraging their complementary strengths. Their differences can create a dynamic and balanced partnership, but it's essential for both partners to appreciate each other's strengths and navigate potential challenges with patience and understanding. With mutual respect and effective communication, the Rat and Ox can build a resilient and fulfilling connection.

Rat and Tiger

Personality Compatibilities

Shared Energy: Both Rats and Tigers are known for their energy, enthusiasm, and active lifestyles. This shared dynamism can lead to a vibrant and exciting relationship where both partners enjoy taking on new challenges and adventures together.

Independence: Rats appreciate their independence, and Tigers, while being social, also value their freedom. This shared desire for autonomy can lead to a relationship where both partners respect each other's space and individuality.

Adventurous Spirit: Tigers are adventurous and courageous, and Rats, while being strategic, can appreciate and support the Tiger's bold initiatives. This can lead to a relationship filled with exciting experiences and shared enthusiasm for exploring new horizons.

Passion: Both signs can be passionate and intense in their pursuits. This shared intensity can contribute to a relationship that is filled with vibrant emotions, deep connections, and mutual understanding.

Personality Differences

Risk Tolerance: Rats tend to be more cautious and calculated in their decision-making, while Tigers may be more inclined to take risks. Balancing these different risk tolerances can be crucial to avoid potential conflicts in decision-making.

Communication Styles: Rats are generally quick-witted and expressive, while Tigers may be more straightforward and direct. Understanding and appreciating each other's communication styles can help minimize misunderstandings and enhance effective communication.

Approach to Conflict: Rats may prefer to strategize and find practical solutions to conflicts, while Tigers may express their emotions more openly. Navigating disagreements involves finding a balance between rational problem-solving and emotional expression.

Social Dynamics: Rats are social creatures who enjoy networking and building connections, while Tigers may be more selective in their social interactions. Finding a balance between socializing and private time is essential for maintaining harmony in the relationship.

In essence, a Rat-Tiger relationship is characterized by shared adventure, social vibrancy, and a dynamic partnership. While their compatibility is evident in their mutual love for excitement, acknowledging and appreciating their differences can lead to a strong and fulfilling connection. With open communication and a willingness to embrace each other's unique qualities, the Rat and Tiger can embark on a thrilling journey of love and growth together.

Rat and Rabbit

Personality Compatibilities

Harmony and Peace: Both Rats and Rabbits generally value harmony and peace in their relationships. This shared desire for tranquility can contribute to a harmonious and stable marriage where both partners work together to maintain a peaceful atmosphere.

Social Compatibility: Rats and Rabbits are often sociable and enjoy the company of others. They may share a mutual interest in socializing, which can lead to an active social life and a wide circle of friends.

Resourcefulness: Rats are known for their intelligence and resourcefulness, and Rabbits are often diplomatic and tactful. This combination of traits can be advantageous when navigating challenges and problem-solving within the marriage.

Family-Oriented: Both signs tend to be family-oriented and value the importance of a close-knit family unit. This shared commitment to family can strengthen their bond and create a supportive environment for their relationship.

Personality Differences

Communication Styles: Rats are generally quick-witted and expressive, while Rabbits may be more reserved and diplomatic in their communication. Understanding and appreciating each other's communication styles can help minimize misunderstandings.

Handling Stress: Rats may approach stress by strategizing and problem-solving, while Rabbits may prefer to avoid conflict and maintain peace. Finding a balance in coping mechanisms during challenging times is crucial for a harmonious relationship.

Risk Tolerance: Rats tend to be more risk-tolerant and adventurous, while Rabbits may be more cautious. Balancing these different risk attitudes can be important when making decisions together.

Independence: Rats value their independence, and Rabbits, while sociable, may also appreciate personal space. Respecting each other's need for independence within the relationship is essential for maintaining balance.

In summary, a Rat-Rabbit relationship is characterized by intellectual harmony, social grace, and a balanced partnership. Their differences add depth to their connection, and with mutual understanding and appreciation, the Rat and Rabbit can create a loving and supportive relationship. Embracing both their shared interests and unique qualities, this duo can embark on a journey of mutual growth and lasting love.

Rat and Dragon

Personality Compatibilities

Shared Energy: Both Rats and Dragons are known for their energy, enthusiasm, and active lifestyles. This shared dynamism can lead to a vibrant and exciting relationship where both partners enjoy taking on new challenges and adventures together.

Intelligence: Rats are intelligent and resourceful, while Dragons are often seen as wise and visionary. This combination of intelligence and wisdom can contribute to effective decision-making and problem-solving within the marriage.

Social Compatibility: Rats and Dragons are generally social creatures who enjoy networking and building connections. They may share a mutual interest in socializing, which can lead to an active social life and shared experiences with friends and family.

Leadership Traits: Both signs possess leadership qualities, with the Rat being strategic and the Dragon being charismatic. This combination can create a dynamic partnership where they complement each other in various aspects of life.

Personality Differences

Approach to Challenges: Rats may prefer a more calculated and strategic approach to challenges, while Dragons may be more impulsive and adventurous. Balancing these different approaches can be crucial to avoid conflicts in decision-making.

Communication Styles: Rats are generally quick-witted and expressive, while Dragons may be more assertive and direct. Understanding and appreciating each other's communication styles can help minimize misunderstandings and enhance effective communication.

Attention to Detail: Rats are detail-oriented and meticulous, while Dragons may focus more on the big picture. Finding a balance between attention to detail and visionary thinking is important for harmony in the relationship.

Independence: Rats value their independence, and Dragons, while confident, may appreciate personal space. Respecting each other's need for independence within the relationship is essential for maintaining balance.

In essence, a Rat-Dragon relationship is characterized by passion, charisma, and a shared zest for life. Their differences can create a dynamic and exciting partnership, but it's essential for both partners to embrace each other's strengths and navigate potential challenges with open communication and mutual respect. With their combined energy and strategic thinking, the Rat and Dragon can embark on a thrilling journey of love and success together.

Rat and Snake

Personality Compatibilities

Resourcefulness: Both Rats and Snakes are known for their resourcefulness and intelligence. This shared trait can contribute to effective problem-solving within the relationship, as they can strategize and navigate challenges together.

Financial Savvy: Rats are generally clever and canny with money, and Snakes are known for their financial acumen. This shared value in financial matters can contribute to effective budgeting, planning, and long-term financial stability for the couple.

Emotional Support: Snakes are often supportive and protective of their loved ones, and Rats can appreciate this loyalty. The Snake's calm and composed nature can provide a sense of emotional stability for the Rat, fostering a strong bond.

Social Compatibility: Rats and Snakes can both appreciate a degree of privacy and are not overly extroverted. This shared preference for a more intimate social circle can contribute to a close-knit relationship.

Personality Differences

Communication Styles: Rats are generally quick-witted and expressive, while Snakes may be more reserved and contemplative. Understanding and appreciating each other's communication styles can help minimize misunderstandings.

Risk Tolerance: Rats tend to be more risk-tolerant and adventurous, while Snakes may be more cautious. Balancing these different risk attitudes can be important when making decisions together.

Social Dynamics: Rats are sociable and enjoy networking, while Snakes may be more selective in their social interactions. Finding a balance between socializing and private time is essential for maintaining harmony in the relationship.

Handling Stress: Rats may approach stress by strategizing and problem-solving, while Snakes may prefer to remain composed and measured. Finding a balance in coping mechanisms during challenging times is crucial for a harmonious relationship.

In summary, a Rat-Snake relationship is characterized by intellectual synergy, social finesse, and a blend of pragmatism with emotional intuition. While their differences add depth to their connection, navigating challenges with patience and open communication will be key to maintaining a strong and fulfilling relationship. With their combined strengths, the Rat and Snake can create a partnership that is both intellectually stimulating and emotionally supportive.

Rat and Horse

Personality Compatibilities

Adventurous Spirit: Both Rats and Horses are generally adventurous and enjoy exploring new opportunities. This shared love for excitement and change can contribute to a dynamic and lively relationship.

Social Compatibility: Rats are sociable creatures who enjoy networking, and Horses are often outgoing and friendly. This shared social inclination can lead to an active and engaging social life for the couple.

Resourcefulness: Rats are known for their resourcefulness, and Horses are usually independent and self-reliant. This combination can create a partnership where both partners contribute their strengths to navigate challenges and pursue goals.

Passion: Horses are passionate individuals, and Rats can appreciate and reciprocate this enthusiasm. This shared intensity can contribute to a relationship filled with vibrant emotions, deep connections, and mutual understanding.

Personality Differences

Approach to Challenges: Rats may prefer a more calculated and strategic approach to challenges, while Horses may be more impulsive and spontaneous. Balancing these different approaches is crucial to avoid conflicts in decision-making.

Communication Styles: Rats are generally quick-witted and expressive, while Horses may be more straightforward and direct. Understanding and appreciating each other's communication styles can help minimize misunderstandings and enhance effective communication.

Commitment to Routine: Rats are comfortable with routines and details, while Horses may seek more variety and freedom. Finding a balance between stability and variety is important for the couple's daily life and long-term plans.

Financial Habits: Rats are usually prudent with money, while Horses may be more inclined to spend impulsively. Navigating differences in financial habits and finding a common ground for budgeting is essential for a harmonious relationship.

In essence, a Rat-Horse relationship is characterized by adventure, social harmony, and a dynamic partnership. While their differences add excitement to their connection, it's essential for both partners to appreciate each other's strengths and navigate potential challenges with open communication and mutual respect. With their combined energy and strategic thinking, the Rat and Horse can embark on a thrilling journey of love and growth together.

Rat and Goat

Personality Compatibilities

Adaptability: Both Rats and Goats can be adaptable and flexible in their approach to life. This shared trait can contribute to a harmonious relationship as they navigate various situations and changes together.

Creativity: Rats are known for their intelligence and resourcefulness, while Goats are often associated with creativity and artistic inclinations. This combination of traits can lead to a relationship where both partners appreciate each other's unique talents and contributions.

Supportive Nature: Goats are generally gentle and nurturing, while Rats can be resourceful and supportive. This combination of qualities can create a nurturing environment in the relationship, where each partner feels cared for and understood.

Harmony: Both Rats and Goats value harmony and may avoid unnecessary conflicts. This shared desire for peace can contribute to a tranquil and stable partnership.

Personality Differences

Communication Styles: Rats are quick-witted and expressive, while Goats may be more reserved and contemplative. Understanding and appreciating each other's communication styles can help minimize misunderstandings.

Financial Habits: Rats are usually prudent with money, while Goats may have a more laid-back approach to finances. Finding a balance between budgeting and enjoying life can be important for financial harmony.

Approach to Challenges: Rats may prefer a more calculated and strategic approach to challenges, while Goats may rely on their emotional intelligence. Combining these approaches can lead to a well-rounded problem-solving dynamic.

Social Dynamics: Rats are sociable and enjoy networking, while Goats may be more selective in their social interactions. Finding a balance between socializing and quiet moments is essential for maintaining harmony in the relationship.

In essence, a Rat-Goat relationship is characterized by emotional harmony, creativity, and adaptability. While their differences add depth to their connection, it's crucial for both partners to appreciate each other's strengths and navigate potential challenges with open communication and mutual respect. With their combined compassion and resourcefulness, the Rat and Goat can create a loving and supportive partnership.

Rat and Monkey

Personality Compatibilities

Intellectual Compatibility: Both Rats and Monkeys are intelligent and quick-witted. This shared intellectual compatibility can lead to engaging conversations and mental stimulation within the relationship.

Adaptability: Rats and Monkeys are generally adaptable and resourceful. Their ability to navigate changes and challenges with agility can contribute to a resilient and dynamic partnership.

Social Compatibility: Rats are sociable and enjoy networking, and Monkeys are often social and charismatic. This shared interest in socializing can lead to an active and vibrant social life for the couple.

Sense of Humor: Both signs are known for their sense of humor. This shared enjoyment of laughter and playfulness can create a lighthearted and enjoyable atmosphere in the relationship.

Personality Differences

Approach to Challenges: Rats may prefer a more calculated and strategic approach to challenges, while Monkeys may be more spontaneous and adventurous. Balancing these different approaches is crucial to avoid conflicts in decision-making.

Communication Styles: Rats are generally quick-witted and expressive, while Monkeys may be more whimsical and humorous. Understanding and appreciating each other's communication styles can help minimize misunderstandings.

Risk Tolerance: Rats tend to be more risk-tolerant and adventurous, while Monkeys may be more cautious. Finding a balance between risk-taking and prudence is important when making decisions together.

Emotional Expression: Rats may approach emotional situations with pragmatism, while Monkeys may inject humor into challenging moments. Navigating these differences in emotional expression requires mutual understanding and empathy.

In essence, a Rat-Monkey relationship is characterized by intellectual synergy, social harmony, and adaptability. While their differences add excitement to their connection, it's crucial for both partners to appreciate each other's strengths and navigate potential challenges with open communication and mutual respect. With their combined energy and strategic thinking, the Rat and Monkey can embark on a lively and fulfilling journey of love and growth together.

Rat and Rooster

Personality Compatibilities

Work Ethic: Both Rats and Roosters are typically hardworking and diligent. This shared work ethic can lead to a harmonious partnership where both partners contribute to their shared goals.

Resourcefulness: Rats are known for their resourcefulness and adaptability, while Roosters are often practical and detail-oriented. This combination of traits can contribute to effective problem-solving and decision-making within the relationship.

Financial Prudence: Rats are usually prudent with money, and Roosters also tend to be financially responsible. This shared value in financial matters can contribute to effective budgeting and long-term financial stability for the couple.

Independence: Rats value their independence, and Roosters, while being cooperative, also appreciate autonomy. Respecting each other's need for personal space and independence within the relationship is essential for maintaining harmony.

Personality Differences

Communication Styles: Rats are generally quick-witted and expressive, while Roosters may be more straightforward and direct. Understanding and appreciating each other's communication styles can help minimize misunderstandings.

Approach to Challenges: Rats may prefer a more calculated and strategic approach to challenges, while Roosters may be more assertive and detail-oriented. Combining these approaches can lead to a well-rounded problem-solving dynamic.

Social Dynamics: Rats are sociable and enjoy networking, while Roosters may be more selective in their social interactions. Finding a balance between socializing and quiet moments is essential for maintaining harmony in the relationship.

Emotional Expression: Rats may approach emotional situations with pragmatism, while Roosters may be more reserved in expressing emotions. Navigating these differences in emotional expression requires open communication and understanding.

In essence, a Rat-Rooster relationship is characterized by shared practicality, hard work, and a commitment to honesty. While their differences add depth to their connection, it's essential for both partners to appreciate each other's strengths and navigate potential challenges with open communication and mutual respect. With their combined diligence and strategic thinking, the Rat and Rooster can create a stable and enduring partnership.

Rat and Dog

Personality Compatibilities

Loyalty: Both Rats and Dogs are known for their loyalty and commitment in relationships. This shared value can create a strong bond, fostering trust and mutual support between the partners.

Communication: Rats are generally quick-witted and expressive, while Dogs are honest and straightforward. These complementary communication styles can contribute to effective and open communication within the relationship.

Supportive Nature: Dogs are often protective and supportive, and Rats appreciate this loyalty. The Dog's caring and nurturing nature can provide emotional support for the Rat, creating a sense of security in the relationship.

Family Orientation: Rats and Dogs are typically family-oriented. This shared commitment to family can lead to a harmonious domestic life and a focus on shared goals for the future.

Personality Differences

Approach to Challenges: Rats may prefer a more calculated and strategic approach to challenges, while Dogs may rely on their instinct and loyalty. Balancing these different approaches is crucial for effective problem-solving within the relationship.

Independence: Rats value their independence, and Dogs, while loyal, may also appreciate personal space. Respecting each other's need for autonomy within the relationship is essential for maintaining balance.

Emotional Expression: Rats may approach emotional situations with pragmatism, while Dogs are known for their emotional sensitivity. Navigating these differences in emotional expression requires understanding and empathy from both partners.

Social Dynamics: Rats are sociable and enjoy networking, while Dogs may be more selective in their social interactions. Finding a balance between socializing and private time is essential for maintaining harmony in the relationship.

In essence, a Rat-Dog relationship is characterized by loyalty, practicality, and a deep emotional connection. While their differences add depth to their connection, it's crucial for both partners to appreciate each other's strengths and navigate potential challenges with open communication and mutual respect. With their shared values of loyalty and practicality, the Rat and Dog can create a stable and enduring partnership filled with love and support.

Rat and Pig

Personality Compatibilities

Harmony: Both Rats and Pigs are generally non-confrontational and value harmony in relationships. This shared desire for peace can contribute to a calm and stable partnership.

Family Orientation: Rats and Pigs are typically family-oriented and prioritize the well-being of their loved ones. This shared commitment to family can lead to a harmonious domestic life and a focus on shared goals for the future.

Emotional Support: Pigs are often nurturing and supportive, and Rats appreciate this caring nature. The Pig's emotional sensitivity can provide a sense of security and understanding for the Rat, fostering a strong emotional bond.

Practicality: Rats are resourceful and practical, and Pigs are generally practical in their approach to life. This shared practicality can contribute to effective problem-solving and decision-making within the relationship.

Personality Differences

Communication Styles: Rats are generally quick-witted and expressive, while Pigs may be more reserved and contemplative. Understanding and appreciating each other's communication styles can help minimize misunderstandings.

Approach to Challenges: Rats may prefer a more calculated and strategic approach to challenges, while Pigs may be more patient and steadier. Combining these approaches can lead to a well-rounded problem-solving dynamic.

Financial Habits: Rats are usually prudent with money, while Pigs may have a more generous approach. Navigating differences in financial habits and finding common ground for budgeting is essential for financial harmony.

Independence: Rats value their independence, and Pigs, while nurturing, may also appreciate personal space. Respecting each other's need for autonomy within the relationship is essential for maintaining balance.

In essence, a Rat-Pig relationship is characterized by kindness, adaptability, and emotional connection. While their differences add depth to their connection, it's crucial for both partners to appreciate each other's strengths and navigate potential challenges with open communication and mutual respect. With their shared values of generosity and adaptability, the Rat and Pig can create a loving and supportive partnership.

Ox and Ox

Personality Compatibilities

Shared Values: Both Oxen are likely to share similar values such as hard work, diligence, and a practical approach to life. This common ground can provide a strong foundation for their relationship.

Work Ethic: Oxen are known for their strong work ethic and perseverance. As a couple, they may jointly commit to their shared goals and work together diligently to achieve them.

Stability: Oxen appreciate stability and security. In a marriage between two Oxen, there may be a mutual desire to create a stable and secure environment for themselves and their family.

Commitment: Oxen are typically loyal and committed partners. In a marriage between two Oxen, there may be a deep sense of commitment and a willingness to work through challenges together.

Personality Differences

Stubbornness: Oxen can be known for their stubbornness, and when two Oxen have differing opinions, it might be challenging to find a middle ground. Both partners may need to practice compromise and flexibility.

Communication Styles: Oxen may not be the most expressive when it comes to emotions. A potential challenge in an Ox-Ox marriage could be a lack of open communication about feelings, requiring effort to create an emotionally nurturing environment.

Routine vs. Variety: Oxen generally appreciate routine and predictability. While this can contribute to stability, it may also lead to a lack of excitement or spontaneity in the relationship. Finding a balance between routine and variety is important for keeping the relationship dynamic.

Adaptability: Oxen may resist change, and when faced with unexpected situations, both partners may need to consciously work on adapting to new circumstances to avoid tension.

In summary, a marriage between two Oxen can have strong foundations based on shared values, commitment, and a mutual work ethic. However, challenges may arise due to stubbornness, a potential lack of emotional expression, and resistance to change. Effective communication, compromise, and a willingness to adapt are crucial for navigating these challenges and maintaining a harmonious and fulfilling relationship.

Ox and Tiger

Personality Compatibilities

Complementary Strengths: Oxen are known for their diligence, reliability, and practicality, while Tigers are often characterized by their courage, enthusiasm, and independent spirit. These differences can complement each other, creating a well-rounded partnership.

Balanced Decision-Making: Oxen are cautious and steady decision-makers, while Tigers may bring more spontaneity and boldness to the relationship. Striking a balance between careful planning and embracing new opportunities can lead to a harmonious decision-making process.

Loyalty: Both the Ox and the Tiger value loyalty and commitment in relationships. This shared value can contribute to a strong bond and a sense of security within the marriage.

Family Focus: Oxen are typically family-oriented, and Tigers, despite their independent nature, can also prioritize family. This shared commitment to family can foster a stable and supportive home environment.

Personality Differences

Communication Styles: Oxen are generally reserved and may prefer practical communication, while Tigers are more expressive and assertive. Understanding and appreciating each other's communication styles are essential for effective interaction.

Approach to Challenges: Oxen prefer a steady and methodical approach to challenges, while Tigers may be more impulsive and bolder. Finding a compromise in their problem-solving strategies can lead to better outcomes.

Independence: Tigers value independence, and Oxen, while appreciating stability, also have an independent streak. Respecting each other's need for personal space and autonomy within the relationship is crucial for maintaining balance.

Risk Tolerance: Tigers are generally more inclined to take risks, while Oxen tend to be more risk-averse. Negotiating and finding a middle ground in their risk tolerance can be essential for avoiding conflicts.

In summary, a marriage between an Ox and a Tiger can have a harmonious blend of stability, loyalty, and adventurous spirit. Effective communication, compromise in decision-making, and respect for each other's independence are key to a successful and fulfilling marriage.

Ox and Rabbit

Personality Compatibilities

Stability: Both Oxen and Rabbits value stability and a peaceful home environment. This shared desire for security can contribute to a calm and steady partnership.

Family Focus: Oxen are typically family-oriented, and Rabbits also prioritize family life. This shared commitment to family values can lead to a harmonious domestic life and a focus on shared goals for the future.

Cautious Approach: Oxen are known for their cautious and methodical approach to life, and Rabbits, while being sociable, also appreciate a more careful and reserved lifestyle. This similarity in approach can contribute to a well-planned and secure future together.

Appreciation for Comfort: Both Oxen and Rabbits generally appreciate comfort and a good standard of living. This shared preference for a comfortable and well-organized home can contribute to domestic harmony.

Personality Differences

Communication Styles: Oxen are generally reserved and may prefer practical communication, while Rabbits can be more diplomatic and sociable. Understanding and appreciating each other's communication styles are important for effective interaction.

Social Dynamics: Rabbits are typically sociable and enjoy socializing, while Oxen may prefer a quieter and more private social life. Finding a balance between socializing and private time is essential for maintaining harmony in the relationship.

Risk Tolerance: Oxen tend to be more risk-averse, preferring a stable and secure approach to life, while Rabbits may be more open to taking calculated risks. Negotiating and finding a middle ground in their risk tolerance can be important for avoiding conflicts.

Decision-Making: Oxen are known for their steady decision-making, while Rabbits may prefer a more diplomatic and flexible approach. Finding a balance between careful consideration and adaptability is essential for mutual understanding.

In summary, a marriage between an Ox and a Rabbit can have a stable and family-focused foundation. Effective communication, understanding each other's social preferences, and finding a balance between caution and adaptability are key to a successful and fulfilling marriage.

Ox and Dragon

Personality Compatibilities

Complementary Strengths: Oxen are known for their diligence, reliability, and practicality, while Dragons are often characterized by their enthusiasm, charisma, and boldness. These differences can complement each other, creating a balanced and dynamic partnership.

Stability: Oxen value stability, and Dragons, while more adventurous, can appreciate the grounding influence of the Ox. This can contribute to a sense of security within the relationship.

Shared Goals: Both Oxen and Dragons can be ambitious and determined. When they align their goals and aspirations, they can work together effectively to achieve success and build a prosperous life.

Loyalty: Both signs value loyalty in relationships. This shared commitment can lead to a strong and lasting bond between the Ox and the Dragon.

Personality Differences

Communication Styles: Oxen are generally reserved and may prefer practical communication, while Dragons are more expressive and assertive. Understanding and appreciating each other's communication styles are essential for effective interaction.

Approach to Challenges: Oxen prefer a steady and methodical approach to challenges, while Dragons may be more spontaneous and bolder. Finding a compromise in their problem-solving strategies can lead to better outcomes.

Social Dynamics: Dragons are often social and enjoy the spotlight, while Oxen may prefer a quieter and more private social life. Negotiating and finding a balance between socializing and private time is important for maintaining harmony.

Risk Tolerance: Dragons are generally more inclined to take risks, while Oxen tend to be more risk-averse. Negotiating and finding a middle ground in their risk tolerance can be essential for avoiding conflicts.

In summary, a marriage between an Ox and a Dragon can have a harmonious blend of stability, ambition, and adventurous spirit. Effective communication, compromise in decision-making, and respect for each other's independence are key to a successful and fulfilling marriage.

Ox and Snake

Personality Compatibilities

Shared Values: Both Oxen and Snakes are generally reserved, thoughtful, and value stability. This shared appreciation for security can contribute to a calm and steady partnership.

Diligence: Oxen are known for their diligent and hardworking nature, and Snakes are often determined and focused. This shared work ethic can lead to a strong commitment to achieving their shared goals.

Practicality: Oxen and Snakes are typically practical and realistic in their approach to life. This shared practicality can contribute to effective problem-solving and decision-making within the relationship.

Loyalty: Both the Ox and the Snake value loyalty and commitment in relationships. This shared value can lead to a strong bond and a sense of trust within the marriage.

Personality Differences

Communication Styles: Oxen are generally reserved and may prefer practical communication, while Snakes can be more diplomatic and intuitive. Understanding and appreciating each other's communication styles are important for effective interaction.

Social Dynamics: Snakes are often charming and sociable, while Oxen may prefer a quieter and more private social life. Finding a balance between socializing and private time is important for maintaining harmony.

Decision-Making: Oxen prefer a steady and methodical approach to decision-making, while Snakes may rely on their intuition. Combining these approaches can lead to a well-rounded problem-solving dynamic.

Financial Habits: Oxen are usually prudent with money, and Snakes may also be financially savvy. This shared value in financial matters can contribute to effective budgeting and long-term financial stability for the couple.

In summary, a marriage between an Ox and a Snake can have a harmonious blend of stability, diligence, and practicality. Effective communication, understanding each other's social preferences, and finding a balance between caution and intuition are key to a successful and fulfilling marriage.

Ox and Horse

Personality Compatibilities

Complementary Strengths: Oxen are known for their diligence, reliability, and practicality, while Horses are often characterized by their enthusiasm, energy, and adventurous spirit. These differences can complement each other, creating a balanced and dynamic partnership.

Stability and Adventure: Oxen value stability, and Horses bring an adventurous and dynamic element to the relationship. Striking a balance between stability and spontaneity can lead to a well-rounded and fulfilling partnership.

Loyalty: Both the Ox and the Horse value loyalty in relationships. This shared commitment can lead to a strong and lasting bond between the partners.

Work Ethic: Oxen are hardworking and diligent, and Horses are usually energetic and determined. When they align their goals and work ethic, they can achieve success and build a prosperous life together.

Personality Differences

Communication Styles: Oxen are generally reserved and may prefer practical communication, while Horses can be more expressive and straightforward. Understanding and appreciating each other's communication styles are important for effective interaction.

Approach to Challenges: Oxen prefer a steady and methodical approach to challenges, while Horses may be more impulsive and bolder. Finding a compromise in their problem-solving strategies can lead to better outcomes.

Social Dynamics: Horses are often social and enjoy new experiences, while Oxen may prefer a quieter and more private social life. Finding a balance between socializing and private time is important for maintaining harmony.

Risk Tolerance: Horses are generally more inclined to take risks, while Oxen tend to be more risk-averse. Negotiating and finding a middle ground in their risk tolerance can be essential for avoiding conflicts.

In summary, a marriage between an Ox and a Horse can have a harmonious blend of stability, loyalty, and adventurous spirit. Effective communication, compromise in decision-making, and respect for each other's independence are key to a successful and fulfilling marriage.

Ox and Goat

Personality Compatibilities

Stability: Both Oxen and Goats appreciate stability and a peaceful home environment. This shared desire for security can contribute to a calm and steady partnership.

Family Focus: Oxen are typically family-oriented, and Goats also prioritize family life. This shared commitment to family values can lead to a harmonious domestic life and a focus on shared goals for the future.

Loyalty: Both the Ox and the Goat value loyalty in relationships. This shared commitment can lead to a strong and lasting bond between the partners.

Work Ethic: Oxen are known for their diligence and hard work, and Goats are often creative and adaptable. When they combine their strengths, they can achieve success and build a prosperous life together.

Personality Differences

Communication Styles: Oxen are generally reserved and may prefer practical communication, while Goats can be more expressive and artistic. Understanding and appreciating each other's communication styles are important for effective interaction.

Social Dynamics: Goats are often sociable and enjoy artistic pursuits, while Oxen may prefer a quieter and more private social life. Finding a balance between socializing and private time is important for maintaining harmony.

Approach to Challenges: Oxen prefer a steady and methodical approach to challenges, while Goats may be more flexible and adaptable. Combining these approaches can lead to a well-rounded problem-solving dynamic.

Financial Habits: Oxen are usually prudent with money, and Goats may have a more laid-back approach. Navigating differences in financial habits and finding common ground for budgeting is essential for financial harmony.

In summary, a marriage between an Ox and a Goat can have a harmonious blend of stability, loyalty, and creativity. Effective communication, understanding each other's social preferences, and finding a balance between caution and adaptability are key to a successful and fulfilling marriage.

Ox and Monkey

Personality Compatibilities

Complementary Strengths: Oxen are known for their diligence, reliability, and practicality, while Monkeys are often characterized by their intelligence, creativity, and quick wit. These differences can complement each other, creating a well-rounded partnership.

Work Ethic: Oxen are hardworking and methodical, and Monkeys are usually energetic and resourceful. When they align their goals and work ethic, they can achieve success and build a prosperous life together.

Stability and Adaptability: Oxen value stability, and Monkeys bring adaptability and versatility to the relationship. Striking a balance between stability and openness to change can lead to a harmonious and dynamic partnership.

Loyalty: Both the Ox and the Monkey value loyalty in relationships. This shared commitment can lead to a strong and lasting bond between the partners.

Personality Differences

Communication Styles: Oxen are generally reserved and may prefer practical communication, while Monkeys are more expressive and communicative. Understanding and appreciating each other's communication styles are important for effective interaction.

Approach to Challenges: Oxen prefer a steady and methodical approach to challenges, while Monkeys may be more spontaneous and quick-thinking. Finding a compromise in their problem-solving strategies can lead to better outcomes.

Social Dynamics: Monkeys are often social and enjoy new experiences, while Oxen may prefer a quieter and more private social life. Negotiating and finding a balance between socializing and private time is important for maintaining harmony.

Risk Tolerance: Monkeys are generally more inclined to take risks, while Oxen tend to be more risk-averse. Negotiating and finding a middle ground in their risk tolerance can be essential for avoiding conflicts.

In summary, a marriage between an Ox and a Monkey can have a harmonious blend of stability, loyalty, and creative intelligence. Effective communication, compromise in decision-making, and respect for each other's independence are key to a successful and fulfilling marriage.

Ox and Rooster

Personality Compatibilities

Work Ethic: Both Oxen and Roosters are known for their hard work and diligence. This shared work ethic can lead to a strong commitment to their shared goals and responsibilities.

Practicality: Oxen and Roosters are generally practical and detail-oriented. This shared practicality can contribute to effective problem-solving and decision-making within the relationship.

Loyalty: Both the Ox and the Rooster value loyalty and commitment in relationships. This shared commitment can lead to a strong and lasting bond between the partners.

Financial Prudence: Oxen are usually prudent with money, and Roosters also tend to be financially responsible. This shared value in financial matters can contribute to effective budgeting and long-term financial stability for the couple.

Personality Differences

Communication Styles: Oxen are generally reserved and may prefer practical communication, while Roosters can be more direct and assertive. Understanding and appreciating each other's communication styles are important for effective interaction.

Social Dynamics: Roosters are often sociable and enjoy being in the spotlight, while Oxen may prefer a quieter and more private social life. Finding a balance between socializing and private time is important for maintaining harmony.

Approach to Challenges: Oxen prefer a steady and methodical approach to challenges, while Roosters may be more assertive and detail-oriented. Combining these approaches can lead to a well-rounded problem-solving dynamic.

Emotional Expression: Oxen may approach emotional situations with pragmatism, while Roosters may be more expressive. Navigating these differences in emotional expression requires understanding and empathy from both partners.

In summary, a marriage between an Ox and a Rooster can have a harmonious blend of stability, loyalty, and practicality. Effective communication, compromise in decision-making, and finding a balance between socializing and private time are key to a successful and fulfilling marriage.

Ox and Dog

Personality Compatibilities

Loyalty: Both Oxen and Dogs are known for their loyalty and commitment in relationships. This shared value can create a strong bond, fostering trust and mutual support between the partners.

Stability: Oxen value stability, and Dogs bring a sense of loyalty and dependability. This shared desire for security can contribute to a calm and steady partnership.

Practicality: Oxen and Dogs are generally practical and realistic in their approach to life. This shared practicality can contribute to effective problem-solving and decision-making within the relationship.

Family Focus: Oxen are typically family-oriented, and Dogs also prioritize family life. This shared commitment to family values can lead to a harmonious domestic life and a focus on shared goals for the future.

Personality Differences

Communication Styles: Oxen are generally reserved and may prefer practical communication, while Dogs can be more expressive and straightforward. Understanding and appreciating each other's communication styles are important for effective interaction.

Social Dynamics: Dogs are often sociable and enjoy companionship, while Oxen may prefer a quieter and more private social life. Finding a balance between socializing and private time is important for maintaining harmony.

Approach to Challenges: Oxen prefer a steady and methodical approach to challenges, while Dogs may be more protective and assertive. Combining these approaches can lead to a well-rounded problem-solving dynamic.

Emotional Expression: Dogs are known for their loyalty and emotional sensitivity, while Oxen may approach emotional situations with pragmatism. Navigating these differences in emotional expression requires open communication and understanding.

In summary, a marriage between an Ox and a Dog can have a harmonious blend of stability, loyalty, and practicality. Effective communication, compromise in decision-making, and finding a balance between socializing and private time are key to a successful and fulfilling marriage.

Ox and Pig

Personality Compatibilities

Stability: Both Oxen and Pigs appreciate stability and a peaceful home environment. This shared desire for security can contribute to a calm and steady partnership.

Family Focus: Oxen are typically family-oriented, and Pigs also prioritize family life. This shared commitment to family values can lead to a harmonious domestic life and a focus on shared goals for the future.

Loyalty: Both the Ox and the Pig value loyalty and commitment in relationships. This shared commitment can lead to a strong and lasting bond between the partners.

Practicality: Oxen and Pigs are generally practical and realistic in their approach to life. This shared practicality can contribute to effective problem-solving and decision-making within the relationship.

Personality Differences

Communication Styles: Oxen are generally reserved and may prefer practical communication, while Pigs can be more expressive and social. Understanding and appreciating each other's communication styles are important for effective interaction.

Social Dynamics: Pigs are often sociable and enjoy socializing, while Oxen may prefer a quieter and more private social life. Finding a balance between socializing and private time is important for maintaining harmony.

Approach to Challenges: Oxen prefer a steady and methodical approach to challenges, while Pigs may be more optimistic and adaptable. Combining these approaches can lead to a well-rounded problem-solving dynamic.

Emotional Expression: Pigs are known for their kindness and emotional sensitivity, while Oxen may approach emotional situations with pragmatism. Navigating these differences in emotional expression requires open communication and understanding.

In summary, a marriage between an Ox and a Pig can have a harmonious blend of stability, loyalty, and practicality. Effective communication, compromise in decision-making, and finding a balance between socializing and private time are key to a successful and fulfilling marriage.

Tiger and Tiger

Personality Compatibilities

Shared Traits: Tigers are often characterized by their boldness, enthusiasm, and adventurous spirit. In a Tiger-Tiger pairing, there can be a strong mutual understanding of these shared traits, creating a dynamic and energetic partnership.

High Energy: Both Tigers bring high levels of energy and passion to the relationship. This shared enthusiasm can contribute to an exciting and lively connection, filled with shared interests and activities.

Courage and Determination: Tigers are known for their courage and determination. In a Tiger-Tiger marriage, there can be a shared commitment to facing challenges head-on and working together to overcome obstacles.

Independence: Tigers value their independence, and in a Tiger-Tiger relationship, there may be a mutual understanding and respect for each other's need for personal space and autonomy.

Personality Differences

Competitiveness: Tigers can be competitive by nature. In a Tiger-Tiger marriage, managing any potential competitiveness and fostering a cooperative spirit is crucial for maintaining harmony.

Impulsiveness: Tigers may be impulsive, and when both partners share this trait, it's important to find a balance between spontaneity and thoughtful decision-making to avoid unnecessary conflicts.

Communication Styles: Tigers can be expressive and assertive. Ensuring effective communication and finding ways to express feelings openly without overwhelming each other is important for a healthy relationship.

Patience: Tigers may have varying levels of patience. It's essential for both partners to practice patience and understanding, especially during challenging times, to avoid unnecessary tension.

In summary, a Tiger-Tiger marriage can be characterized by shared energy, enthusiasm, and a willingness to face challenges together. However, managing potential areas of competition, impulsiveness, and ensuring effective communication are key to fostering a harmonious and fulfilling relationship.

Tiger and Rabbit

Personality Compatibilities

Balance of Energies: Tigers are often characterized by their boldness, enthusiasm, and adventurous spirit, while Rabbits are known for their gentleness, diplomacy, and sensitivity. These differences can create a harmonious balance, with the Tiger's energy complementing the Rabbit's more serene nature.

Mutual Attraction: Tigers are often drawn to the Rabbit's charm, grace, and refined nature. In turn, Rabbits may appreciate the Tiger's dynamic and confident approach to life, finding it exciting and invigorating.

Supportive Relationship: Tigers and Rabbits can create a supportive dynamic where the Rabbit's diplomatic and calming influence helps soothe any potential conflicts that may arise from the Tiger's boldness. This complementary support can contribute to a stable and nurturing relationship.

Shared Goals: Both Tigers and Rabbits can value security and a comfortable home life. When they align their goals and aspirations, they can work together effectively to build a stable and happy future.

Personality Differences

Communication Styles: Tigers are expressive and assertive, while Rabbits tend to be more diplomatic and reserved. Navigating these differences in communication styles requires understanding and effective communication from both partners.

Risk Tolerance: Tigers are generally more inclined to take risks, while Rabbits may be more risk-averse. Finding a middle ground in their risk tolerance is important for avoiding conflicts, especially in decision-making.

Social Dynamics: Tigers may enjoy a more active and outgoing social life, while Rabbits may prefer a quieter and more intimate setting. Finding a balance between socializing and private time is crucial for maintaining harmony.

Handling Stress: Tigers may confront stress more directly, while Rabbits might withdraw or seek a peaceful environment. Understanding each other's coping mechanisms is vital for providing support during challenging times.

In summary, a marriage between a Tiger and a Rabbit can have a harmonious blend of energy, support, and complementary qualities. Effective communication, finding common ground in decision-making, and respecting each other's need for both excitement and tranquility are key to a successful and fulfilling marriage.

Tiger and Dragon

Personality Compatibilities

Shared Energies: Both Tigers and Dragons are characterized by boldness, enthusiasm, and a zest for life. This shared energy can create a dynamic and exciting partnership filled with mutual passion and adventure.

Mutual Attraction: Tigers may be drawn to the Dragon's charisma, confidence, and powerful presence. In turn, Dragons might appreciate the Tiger's fiery and independent nature, finding it invigorating.

Courage and Determination: Tigers and Dragons are known for their courage and determination. In a Tiger-Dragon marriage, there can be a shared commitment to facing challenges head-on and working together to overcome obstacles.

Shared Goals: Both signs can be ambitious and goal-oriented. When aligned, their shared determination and focus can lead to success in their endeavors and a thriving partnership.

Personality Differences

Communication Styles: Tigers are expressive and assertive, while Dragons may be more commanding and authoritative. Navigating these differences in communication styles requires understanding and effective communication from both partners.

Handling Conflicts: Tigers may confront conflicts more directly, while Dragons might prefer to maintain a sense of pride and avoid confrontation. Finding a balance in handling conflicts is crucial for maintaining harmony.

Social Dynamics: Both Tigers and Dragons can enjoy a lively social life, but Dragons might be more inclined to take on leadership roles. Finding a balance between sharing the spotlight and supporting each other's individuality is important.

Independence: Tigers and Dragons both value independence. While this shared trait can contribute to a dynamic relationship, finding ways to support each other's freedom and individual pursuits is essential.

In summary, a marriage between a Tiger and a Dragon can be passionate, adventurous, and filled with shared goals. Effective communication, mutual respect for each other's independence, and understanding each other's approaches to conflicts are key to a successful and fulfilling marriage.

Tiger and Snake

Personality Compatibilities

Attraction: Tigers may be drawn to the Snake's charm, sophistication, and mysterious aura. In turn, Snakes might appreciate the Tiger's boldness, energy, and passionate nature, finding it invigorating.

Balancing Energies: Tigers are known for their boldness and enthusiasm, while Snakes are often more calculating and strategic. This combination can create a balance, where the Snake's wisdom and planning complement the Tiger's dynamic and energetic approach.

Protective Instincts: Tigers are protective by nature, and Snakes may appreciate the sense of security and support that the Tiger provides. This shared value can contribute to a strong and nurturing partnership.

Individuality: Both Tigers and Snakes value their independence and individuality. When they respect and support each other's freedom, it can lead to a harmonious coexistence within the relationship.

Personality Differences

Communication Styles: Tigers are expressive and assertive, while Snakes can be more diplomatic and intuitive. Navigating these differences in communication styles requires understanding and effective communication from both partners.

Handling Conflicts: Tigers may confront conflicts more directly, while Snakes might prefer a more subtle and calculated approach. Finding a balance in handling conflicts is crucial for maintaining harmony.

Social Dynamics: Tigers may enjoy a more active and outgoing social life, while Snakes may prefer a smaller, more intimate circle. Finding a balance between socializing and private time is important for maintaining harmony.

Trust and Jealousy: Snakes value trust and loyalty, and Tigers may need to be mindful of potential jealousy issues. Building trust through open communication and reassurance is essential in overcoming any insecurities.

In summary, a marriage between a Tiger and a Snake can have a harmonious blend of energy, protection, and strategic thinking. Effective communication, mutual respect for each other's independence, and understanding each other's approaches to conflicts are key to a successful and fulfilling marriage.

Tiger and Horse

Personality Compatibilities

Shared Energies: Tigers and Horses are both characterized by boldness, enthusiasm, and an adventurous spirit. This shared energy can create a dynamic and exciting partnership filled with mutual passion and zest for life.

Mutual Attraction: Tigers may be drawn to the Horse's energy, independence, and love for freedom. In turn, Horses might appreciate the Tiger's dynamic nature, finding it invigorating and exhilarating.

Courage and Determination: Both Tigers and Horses are known for their courage and determination. In a Tiger-Horse marriage, there can be a shared commitment to facing challenges head-on and working together to overcome obstacles.

Shared Goals: Tigers and Horses can be ambitious and goal-oriented. When aligned, their shared determination and focus can lead to success in their endeavors and a thriving partnership.

Personality Differences

Communication Styles: Tigers are expressive and assertive, while Horses may be more direct and straightforward. Navigating these differences in communication styles requires understanding and effective communication from both partners.

Handling Conflicts: Tigers may confront conflicts more directly, while Horses might prefer a more spontaneous and open approach. Finding a balance in handling conflicts is crucial for maintaining harmony.

Social Dynamics: Both Tigers and Horses enjoy an active social life, but Horses may be more spontaneous and outgoing. Finding a balance between socializing and private time is important for maintaining harmony.

Independence: Tigers and Horses both value their independence. While this shared trait can contribute to a dynamic relationship, finding ways to support each other's freedom and individual pursuits is essential.

In summary, a marriage between a Tiger and a Horse can be passionate, adventurous, and filled with shared goals. Effective communication, mutual respect for each other's independence, and understanding each other's approaches to conflicts are key to a successful and fulfilling marriage.

Tiger and Goat

Personality Compatibilities

Balance of Energies: Tigers are often characterized by boldness, enthusiasm, and an adventurous spirit, while Goats are known for their gentleness, creativity, and sensitivity. This combination can create a harmonious balance, where the Tiger's energy complements the Goat's more serene nature.

Mutual Attraction: Tigers may be drawn to the Goat's charm, grace, and artistic nature. In turn, Goats might appreciate the Tiger's dynamic and confident approach to life, finding it invigorating.

Protective Instincts: Tigers are protective by nature, and Goats may appreciate the sense of security and support that the Tiger provides. This shared value can contribute to a strong and nurturing partnership.

Individuality: Both Tigers and Goats value their independence and individuality. When they respect and support each other's freedom, it can lead to a harmonious coexistence within the relationship.

Personality Differences

Communication Styles: Tigers are expressive and assertive, while Goats can be more diplomatic and reserved. Navigating these differences in communication styles requires understanding and effective communication from both partners.

Handling Conflicts: Tigers may confront conflicts more directly, while Goats might prefer a more subtle and gentle approach. Finding a balance in handling conflicts is crucial for maintaining harmony.

Social Dynamics: Tigers may enjoy a more active and outgoing social life, while Goats may prefer a smaller, more intimate circle. Finding a balance between socializing and private time is important for maintaining harmony.

Risk Tolerance: Tigers are generally more inclined to take risks, while Goats may be more cautious. Negotiating and finding a middle ground in their risk tolerance is important for avoiding conflicts, especially in decision-making.

In summary, a marriage between a Tiger and a Goat can have a harmonious blend of energy, protection, and artistic sensitivity. Effective communication, mutual respect for each other's independence, and understanding each other's approaches to conflicts are key to a successful and fulfilling marriage.

Tiger and Monkey

Personality Compatibilities

Shared Energies: Tigers and Monkeys are characterized by boldness, enthusiasm, and an adventurous spirit. This shared energy can create a dynamic and exciting partnership filled with mutual passion and zest for life.

Mutual Attraction: Tigers may be drawn to the Monkey's intelligence, wit, and lively nature. In turn, Monkeys might appreciate the Tiger's dynamic and confident approach to life, finding it invigorating and entertaining.

Sense of Humor: Both Tigers and Monkeys tend to have a good sense of humor and enjoy playful banter. This shared love for laughter can contribute to a light-hearted and enjoyable relationship.

Curiosity and Creativity: Monkeys are known for their curiosity and creativity, which can complement the Tiger's boldness and adventurous spirit. Together, they can explore new ideas and experiences.

Personality Differences

Communication Styles: Tigers are expressive and assertive, while Monkeys are communicative and quick-witted. Navigating these differences in communication styles requires understanding and effective communication from both partners.

Handling Conflicts: Tigers may confront conflicts more directly, while Monkeys might use humor and cleverness to diffuse tension. Finding a balance in handling conflicts is crucial for maintaining harmony.

Social Dynamics: Monkeys are often sociable and enjoy being in the spotlight, while Tigers may prefer a more straightforward and direct approach. Finding a balance between sharing the spotlight and supporting each other's individuality is important.

Risk Tolerance: Monkeys are generally more inclined to take risks, while Tigers may also enjoy a bit of adventure. Negotiating and finding a middle ground in their risk tolerance is important for avoiding conflicts, especially in decision-making.

In summary, a marriage between a Tiger and a Monkey can be passionate, playful, and filled with shared adventures. Effective communication, mutual respect for each other's individuality, and understanding each other's approaches to conflicts are key to a successful and fulfilling marriage.

Tiger and Rooster

Personality Compatibilities

Complementary Strengths: Tigers are often characterized by boldness, enthusiasm, and an adventurous spirit, while Roosters are known for their practicality, diligence, and attention to detail. These differences can create a well-rounded partnership where the Tiger's energy complements the Rooster's more grounded and organized nature.

Work Ethic: Both Tigers and Roosters are hardworking and dedicated. This shared work ethic can lead to a strong commitment to their shared goals and responsibilities.

Protection and Support: Tigers are protective by nature, and Roosters may appreciate the Tiger's sense of security and support. This shared value can contribute to a strong and nurturing partnership.

Individuality: Both Tigers and Roosters value their independence and individuality. When they respect and support each other's freedom, it can lead to a harmonious coexistence within the relationship.

Personality Differences

Communication Styles: Tigers are expressive and assertive, while Roosters are direct and may emphasize practical communication. Navigating these differences in communication styles requires understanding and effective communication from both partners.

Handling Conflicts: Tigers may confront conflicts more directly, while Roosters might prefer a more organized and structured approach. Finding a balance in handling conflicts is crucial for maintaining harmony.

Social Dynamics: Tigers may enjoy a more active and outgoing social life, while Roosters may prefer a smaller, more intimate circle. Finding a balance between socializing and private time is important for maintaining harmony.

Approach to Challenges: Tigers may be more spontaneous and risk-taking, while Roosters are often methodical and cautious. Combining these approaches can lead to a well-rounded problem-solving dynamic.

In summary, a marriage between a Tiger and a Rooster can have a harmonious blend of energy, protection, and practicality. Effective communication, mutual respect for each other's independence, and understanding each other's approaches to conflicts are key to a successful and fulfilling marriage.

Tiger and Dog

Personality Compatibilities

Loyalty: Both Tigers and Dogs are known for their loyalty and commitment in relationships. This shared value can create a strong bond, fostering trust and mutual support between the partners.

Protective Instincts: Tigers are protective by nature, and Dogs are often loyal and protective as well. This shared instinct can contribute to a strong sense of security and support within the marriage.

Shared Goals: Tigers and Dogs can be ambitious and goal-oriented. When aligned, their shared determination and focus can lead to success in their endeavors and a thriving partnership.

Individuality: Both Tigers and Dogs value their independence. When they respect and support each other's freedom, it can lead to a harmonious coexistence within the relationship.

Personality Differences

Communication Styles: Tigers are expressive and assertive, while Dogs may be more straightforward and loyal. Navigating these differences in communication styles requires understanding and effective communication from both partners.

Handling Conflicts: Tigers may confront conflicts more directly, while Dogs might approach conflicts with a sense of loyalty and protectiveness. Finding a balance in handling conflicts is crucial for maintaining harmony.

Social Dynamics: Tigers may enjoy a more active and outgoing social life, while Dogs may prefer a smaller, more intimate circle. Finding a balance between socializing and private time is important for maintaining harmony.

Approach to Challenges: Tigers may be more spontaneous and risk-taking, while Dogs are often cautious and protective. Combining these approaches can lead to a well-rounded problem-solving dynamic.

In summary, a marriage between a Tiger and a Dog can have a harmonious blend of loyalty, protection, and shared goals. Effective communication, mutual respect for each other's independence, and understanding each other's approaches to conflicts are key to a successful and fulfilling marriage.

Tiger and Pig

Personality Compatibilities

Attraction: Tigers may be drawn to the Pig's kindness, generosity, and gentle nature. In turn, Pigs might appreciate the Tiger's dynamic and confident approach to life, finding it invigorating.

Protective Instincts: Tigers are protective by nature, and Pigs may appreciate the sense of security and support that the Tiger provides. This shared value can contribute to a strong and nurturing partnership.

Mutual Respect: Both Tigers and Pigs can have a mutual respect for each other's individuality. When they appreciate and support each other's freedom, it can lead to a harmonious coexistence within the relationship.

Shared Goals: Tigers and Pigs can both be ambitious and goal-oriented. When aligned, their shared determination and focus can lead to success in their endeavors and a thriving partnership.

Personality Differences

Communication Styles: Tigers are expressive and assertive, while Pigs are often diplomatic and gentle. Navigating these differences in communication styles requires understanding and effective communication from both partners.

Handling Conflicts: Tigers may confront conflicts more directly, while Pigs might prefer a more peaceful and cooperative approach. Finding a balance in handling conflicts is crucial for maintaining harmony.

Social Dynamics: Tigers may enjoy a more active and outgoing social life, while Pigs may prefer a quieter and more intimate circle. Finding a balance between socializing and private time is important for maintaining harmony.

Approach to Challenges: Tigers may be more spontaneous and risk-taking, while Pigs are often more patient and cautious. Combining these approaches can lead to a well-rounded problem-solving dynamic.

In summary, a marriage between a Tiger and a Pig can have a harmonious blend of protection, mutual respect, and shared goals. Effective communication, compromise in handling conflicts, and finding a balance between socializing and private time are key to a successful and fulfilling marriage.

Rabbit and Rabbit

Personality Compatibilities

Gentleness and Sensitivity: Rabbits are known for their gentle and sensitive nature. In a Rabbit-Rabbit pairing, there can be a shared understanding and appreciation for each other's emotional needs, creating a nurturing and supportive environment.

Harmony and Peace: Rabbits generally value harmony and peace. In a Rabbit-Rabbit relationship, there can be a mutual desire for a calm and serene atmosphere, contributing to a harmonious partnership.

Creativity: Rabbits are often creative and artistic. In a Rabbit-Rabbit marriage, there can be shared interests in artistic pursuits, fostering a creative and imaginative aspect to their relationship.

Politeness and Courtesy: Rabbits tend to be polite and courteous. In a Rabbit-Rabbit pairing, there may be a natural inclination towards kindness and consideration, creating a polite and respectful partnership.

Personality Differences

Decision-Making: Rabbits may sometimes struggle with decision-making due to their gentle and hesitant nature. In a Rabbit-Rabbit relationship, making decisions may require extra effort, and finding a balance in taking initiative is essential.

Avoidance of Conflict: Rabbits may avoid confrontation to maintain harmony. While this can be positive, addressing conflicts directly and finding constructive solutions is crucial for long-term relationship health.

Assertiveness: Rabbits may lack assertiveness, and in a Rabbit-Rabbit marriage, effective communication and the ability to express needs and desires openly is important for preventing misunderstandings.

Handling Stress: Rabbits may find it challenging to handle stress. In a Rabbit-Rabbit relationship, developing coping mechanisms and supporting each other during challenging times is crucial.

In summary, a marriage between two Rabbits can have a harmonious and gentle quality, with shared values of peace, creativity, and sensitivity. However, addressing potential challenges in decision-making, assertiveness, and conflict resolution is important for maintaining a healthy and fulfilling relationship.

Rabbit and Dragon

Personality Compatibilities

Charm and Attraction: Rabbits are often drawn to the Dragon's charisma, confidence, and powerful presence. In turn, Dragons might appreciate the Rabbit's gentle and nurturing nature, finding it comforting.

Creativity and Inspiration: Rabbits are generally creative and artistic, while Dragons exude energy and inspiration. This combination can lead to a dynamic partnership where the Rabbit's creativity is complemented by the Dragon's enthusiasm.

Supportive Roles: Dragons, known for their leadership qualities, can provide a sense of security and support to the more reserved and gentle Rabbit. The Rabbit, in turn, can offer emotional support and understanding to the Dragon.

Harmony: Both Rabbits and Dragons can appreciate a harmonious environment. Finding common ground in maintaining a peaceful and balanced home life can contribute to the overall well-being of the relationship.

Personality Differences

Communication Styles: Rabbits are often diplomatic and tactful, while Dragons can be more direct and assertive. Navigating these differences in communication styles requires understanding and effective communication from both partners.

Handling Conflicts: Rabbits may avoid conflict to maintain harmony, while Dragons might confront issues head-on. Balancing the need for open communication with the Rabbit's preference for peace is crucial for avoiding misunderstandings.

Independence: Dragons value independence and may have a more dominant personality, while Rabbits appreciate a more gentle and supportive approach. Respecting each other's independence and finding a balance in decision-making is essential.

Social Dynamics: Dragons may enjoy a more active and outgoing social life, while Rabbits may prefer a quieter setting. Finding a compromise in social activities can contribute to a harmonious relationship.

In summary, a marriage between a Rabbit and a Dragon can be a blend of charm, creativity, and support. Effective communication, understanding and respecting each other's differences, and finding a balance in decision-making are key to a successful and fulfilling marriage.

Rabbit and Snake

Personality Compatibilities

Diplomacy: Both Rabbits and Snakes can be diplomatic and tactful in their interactions. This shared trait can contribute to a relationship where conflicts are approached with sensitivity and a desire for resolution.

Emotional Depth: Rabbits are known for their emotional depth, while Snakes can be intuitive and perceptive. This combination can create a profound emotional connection, where both partners understand and support each other on a deeper level.

Shared Interests: Rabbits and Snakes may appreciate the finer things in life. Shared interests in art, culture, and aesthetics can contribute to a harmonious and enriching partnership.

Independence: Both Rabbits and Snakes value their independence. When they respect and support each other's freedom, it can lead to a harmonious coexistence within the relationship.

Personality Differences

Communication Styles: Rabbits are often diplomatic, while Snakes may be more reserved and secretive. Navigating these differences in communication styles requires understanding and effective communication from both partners.

Handling Conflicts: Rabbits may avoid conflict to maintain harmony, while Snakes might prefer a more strategic and calculated approach. Finding a balance in addressing conflicts is crucial for maintaining harmony.

Social Dynamics: Rabbits may enjoy a more active and outgoing social life, while Snakes may prefer a smaller, more intimate circle. Finding a balance between socializing and private time is important for maintaining harmony.

Approach to Challenges: Rabbits may be more sensitive, while Snakes can be resilient and calculated. Combining these approaches can lead to a well-rounded problem-solving dynamic.

In summary, a marriage between a Rabbit and a Snake can have a harmonious blend of diplomacy, emotional depth, and shared interests. Effective communication, compromise in handling conflicts, and finding a balance between socializing and private time are key to a successful and fulfilling marriage.

Rabbit and Horse

Personality Compatibilities

Balance of Energies: Rabbits are often characterized by their gentleness, sensitivity, and love for peace, while Horses are known for their energy, enthusiasm, and adventurous spirit. This combination can create a harmonious balance, where the Rabbit's calm nature complements the Horse's more active energy.

Mutual Attraction: Rabbits may be drawn to the Horse's vitality, independence, and love for freedom. In turn, Horses might appreciate the Rabbit's gentle and nurturing nature, finding it comforting.

Supportive Roles: Rabbits, with their diplomatic and caring approach, can provide emotional support to the more impulsive and energetic Horse. The Horse, in turn, can bring excitement and enthusiasm into the relationship.

Harmony: Both Rabbits and Horses can appreciate harmony, albeit in different ways. Finding common ground in maintaining a peaceful and balanced home life can contribute to the overall well-being of the relationship.

Personality Differences

Communication Styles: Rabbits are often diplomatic and tactful, while Horses may be more direct and assertive. Navigating these differences in communication styles requires understanding and effective communication from both partners.

Handling Conflicts: Rabbits may avoid conflict to maintain harmony, while Horses might confront issues more directly. Finding a balance in addressing conflicts is crucial for maintaining harmony.

Social Dynamics: Horses may enjoy a more active and outgoing social life, while Rabbits may prefer a quieter and more intimate setting. Finding a balance between socializing and private time is important for maintaining harmony.

Approach to Challenges: Rabbits may be more cautious, while Horses are often more spontaneous. Combining these approaches can lead to a well-rounded problem-solving dynamic.

In summary, a marriage between a Rabbit and a Horse can have a harmonious blend of balance, support, and mutual attraction. Effective communication, understanding and respecting each other's differences, and finding a balance between socializing and private time are key to a successful and fulfilling marriage.

Rabbit and Goat

Personality Compatibilities

Harmony and Peace: Both Rabbits and Goats value harmony and peace. In a Rabbit-Goat relationship, there can be a shared desire for a calm and serene atmosphere, contributing to a harmonious partnership.

Gentleness: Rabbits are known for their gentle and sensitive nature, and Goats share a similar gentleness. This shared trait can create a nurturing and supportive environment within the relationship.

Artistic and Creative Interests: Rabbits and Goats are often associated with artistic and creative interests. Shared hobbies and appreciation for aesthetics can contribute to a fulfilling and enriching partnership.

Supportive Roles: Both Rabbits and Goats may appreciate a supportive role in the relationship. There can be a mutual understanding and willingness to provide emotional support to each other.

Personality Differences

Communication Styles: Rabbits are often diplomatic and tactful, while Goats may be more reserved and introspective. Navigating these differences in communication styles requires understanding and effective communication from both partners.

Handling Conflicts: Rabbits may avoid conflict to maintain harmony, while Goats might prefer a more passive or indirect approach. Finding a balance in addressing conflicts is crucial for maintaining harmony.

Social Dynamics: Rabbits may enjoy a more active and outgoing social life, while Goats may prefer a smaller, more intimate circle. Finding a balance between socializing and private time is important for maintaining harmony.

Approach to Challenges: Rabbits may be more cautious, while Goats might rely on intuition. Combining these approaches can lead to a well-rounded problem-solving dynamic.

In summary, a marriage between a Rabbit and a Goat can have a harmonious blend of gentleness, artistic interests, and a shared desire for peace. Effective communication, understanding and respecting each other's differences, and finding a balance between socializing and private time are key to a successful and fulfilling marriage.

Rabbit and Monkey

Personality Compatibilities

Charm and Attraction: Rabbits may be drawn to the Monkey's intelligence, wit, and lively nature. In turn, Monkeys might appreciate the Rabbit's gentle and nurturing qualities, finding them comforting.

Creativity and Playfulness: Both Rabbits and Monkeys can possess creativity and playfulness. Shared interests in artistic pursuits and a love for fun and entertainment can contribute to a dynamic and enjoyable partnership.

Supportive Roles: Rabbits, with their diplomatic and caring approach, can provide emotional support to the more energetic and sometimes mischievous Monkey. The Monkey, in turn, can bring excitement and enthusiasm into the relationship.

Harmony: Both Rabbits and Monkeys may appreciate harmony in their relationships, albeit in different ways. Finding common ground in maintaining a peaceful and balanced home life can contribute to the overall well-being of the relationship.

Personality Differences

Communication Styles: Rabbits are often diplomatic and tactful, while Monkeys are communicative and quick-witted. Navigating these differences in communication styles requires understanding and effective communication from both partners.

Handling Conflicts: Rabbits may avoid conflict to maintain harmony, while Monkeys might approach conflicts with a sense of humor and cleverness. Finding a balance in handling conflicts is crucial for maintaining harmony.

Social Dynamics: Monkeys are often sociable and enjoy being in the spotlight, while Rabbits may prefer a quieter setting. Finding a compromise in social activities can contribute to a harmonious relationship.

Approach to Challenges: Rabbits may be more sensitive, while Monkeys can be resilient and adaptable. Combining these approaches can lead to a well-rounded problem-solving dynamic.

In summary, a marriage between a Rabbit and a Monkey can have a harmonious blend of charm, creativity, and support. Effective communication, understanding and respecting each other's differences, and finding a balance between socializing and private time are key to a successful and fulfilling marriage.

Rabbit and Rooster

Personality Compatibilities

Balanced Energies: Rabbits are often characterized by their gentleness, sensitivity, and love for peace, while Roosters are known for their practicality, diligence, and attention to detail. This combination can create a balanced partnership where the Rabbit's calm nature complements the Rooster's more organized and focused energy.

Harmony: Both Rabbits and Roosters can appreciate harmony, albeit in different ways. Finding common ground in maintaining a peaceful and balanced home life can contribute to the overall well-being of the relationship.

Supportive Roles: Rabbits, with their diplomatic and caring approach, can provide emotional support to the more assertive and disciplined Rooster. The Rooster, in turn, can bring structure and order into the relationship.

Attention to Aesthetics: Rabbits and Roosters may appreciate aesthetics in different ways. While Rabbits are often associated with artistic interests, Roosters may focus on the practical and visual aspects of their surroundings. Finding common ground in their appreciation for beauty can enrich the relationship.

Personality Differences

Communication Styles: Rabbits are often diplomatic and tactful, while Roosters are direct and straightforward. Navigating these differences in communication styles requires understanding and effective communication from both partners.

Handling Conflicts: Rabbits may avoid conflict to maintain harmony, while Roosters might confront issues head-on. Finding a balance in addressing conflicts is crucial for maintaining harmony.

Social Dynamics: Rabbits may enjoy a more active and outgoing social life, while Roosters may prefer a smaller, more intimate circle. Finding a compromise in social activities can contribute to a harmonious relationship.

Approach to Challenges: Rabbits may be more sensitive, while Roosters can be practical and analytical. Combining these approaches can lead to a well-rounded problem-solving dynamic.

In summary, a marriage between a Rabbit and a Rooster can have a harmonious blend of balance, support, and attention to aesthetics. Effective communication, understanding and respecting each other's differences, and finding a balance between socializing and private time are key to a successful and fulfilling marriage.

Rabbit and Dog

Personality Compatibilities

Harmony and Peace: Both Rabbits and Dogs value harmony and peace. In a Rabbit-Dog relationship, there can be a shared desire for a calm and serene atmosphere, contributing to a harmonious partnership.

Gentleness: Rabbits are known for their gentle and sensitive nature, and Dogs share a similar gentleness. This shared trait can create a nurturing and supportive environment within the relationship.

Loyalty: Both Rabbits and Dogs are known for their loyalty and commitment in relationships. This shared value can create a strong bond, fostering trust and mutual support between the partners.

Supportive Roles: Rabbits, with their diplomatic and caring approach, can provide emotional support to the loyal and protective Dog. The Dog, in turn, can offer a sense of security and dependability.

Personality Differences

Communication Styles: Rabbits are often diplomatic and tactful, while Dogs may be more straightforward and loyal. Navigating these differences in communication styles requires understanding and effective communication from both partners.

Handling Conflicts: Rabbits may avoid conflict to maintain harmony, while Dogs might confront issues with a sense of loyalty and protectiveness. Finding a balance in addressing conflicts is crucial for maintaining harmony.

Social Dynamics: Dogs may have a more reserved and cautious approach to socializing, while Rabbits may enjoy a more active and outgoing social life. Finding a balance between socializing and private time is important for maintaining harmony.

Approach to Challenges: Rabbits may be more sensitive, while Dogs are often resilient and protective. Combining these approaches can lead to a well-rounded problem-solving dynamic.

In summary, a marriage between a Rabbit and a Dog can have a harmonious blend of gentleness, loyalty, and support. Effective communication, understanding and respecting each other's differences, and finding a balance between socializing and private time are key to a successful and fulfilling marriage.

Rabbit and Pig

Personality Compatibilities

Harmony and Peace: Both Rabbits and Pigs value harmony and peace. In a Rabbit-Pig relationship, there can be a shared desire for a calm and serene atmosphere, contributing to a harmonious partnership.

Gentleness: Rabbits are known for their gentle and sensitive nature, and Pigs share a similar gentleness. This shared trait can create a nurturing and supportive environment within the relationship.

Creativity and Aesthetics: Rabbits and Pigs are often associated with artistic interests. Shared hobbies and an appreciation for beauty and aesthetics can contribute to a fulfilling and enriching partnership.

Supportive Roles: Rabbits, with their diplomatic and caring approach, can provide emotional support to the compassionate and generous Pig. The Pig, in turn, can offer warmth and support to the Rabbit.

Personality Differences

Communication Styles: Rabbits are often diplomatic and tactful, while Pigs may be more straightforward and open. Navigating these differences in communication styles requires understanding and effective communication from both partners.

Handling Conflicts: Rabbits may avoid conflict to maintain harmony, while Pigs might approach issues with a sense of generosity and understanding. Finding a balance in addressing conflicts is crucial for maintaining harmony.

Social Dynamics: Rabbits may enjoy a more active and outgoing social life, while Pigs may prefer a quieter and more intimate circle. Finding a compromise in social activities can contribute to a harmonious relationship.

Approach to Challenges: Rabbits may be more sensitive, while Pigs are often patient and adaptable. Combining these approaches can lead to a well-rounded problem-solving dynamic.

In summary, a marriage between a Rabbit and a Pig can have a harmonious blend of gentleness, creativity, and support. Effective communication, understanding and respecting each other's differences, and finding a balance between socializing and private time are key to a successful and fulfilling marriage.

Dragon and Dragon

Personality Compatibilities

Shared Energy and Ambition: Dragons are known for their energy, charisma, and ambition. In a Dragon-Dragon relationship, there can be a shared drive for success and achievement, leading to a dynamic and goal-oriented partnership.

Enthusiasm: Dragons are often enthusiastic and passionate. The shared enthusiasm can create a vibrant and lively atmosphere in the relationship, with both partners supporting each other's pursuits and dreams.

Creativity: Dragons are associated with creativity and innovation. In a Dragon-Dragon marriage, there can be a shared interest in exploring new ideas and expressing creativity, leading to a dynamic and exciting partnership.

Mutual Understanding: Both Dragons may share similar characteristics and understand each other's desires for independence and personal growth. This understanding can contribute to mutual respect and support within the relationship.

Personality Differences

Dominance: Dragons can be dominant individuals. In a Dragon-Dragon relationship, finding a balance between asserting individual opinions and allowing space for the partner's perspective is crucial for maintaining harmony.

Communication Styles: Dragons may have a direct and assertive communication style. Navigating potential clashes in communication and ensuring effective dialogue requires mutual understanding and respect.

Handling Conflicts: Dragons may confront conflicts more directly. Learning to approach conflicts with patience and understanding is important to prevent unnecessary tension in the relationship.

Attention to Detail: Dragons may focus on the bigger picture and may not pay meticulous attention to details. In a Dragon-Dragon marriage, finding a balance between vision and practicality can contribute to effective decision-making.

In summary, a marriage between two Dragons can be dynamic, passionate, and goal-oriented. While there are shared traits and ambitions, managing potential challenges related to dominance, communication styles, and attention to detail is essential for maintaining a healthy and fulfilling relationship.

Dragon and Snake

Personality Compatibilities

Shared Ambition: Dragons are known for their energy, charisma, and ambition, and Snakes can be strategic and goal-oriented. In a Dragon-Snake relationship, there can be a shared drive for success and a mutual understanding of each other's ambitions.

Charismatic Presence: Both Dragons and Snakes can possess a charismatic presence. This shared quality can enhance their social interactions and contribute to a dynamic and engaging partnership.

Adaptability: Snakes are often adaptable and strategic, while Dragons can be versatile. This combination can result in a relationship that navigates challenges effectively and embraces change when necessary.

Appreciation for Beauty: Dragons and Snakes may share an appreciation for aesthetics and beauty. This common interest can lead to a harmonious and enriching partnership, especially in the areas of art and culture.

Personality Differences

Communication Styles: Dragons may have a more direct and assertive communication style, while Snakes are often more reserved and diplomatic. Navigating these differences requires mutual understanding and effective communication from both partners.

Handling Conflicts: Dragons may confront conflicts more directly, while Snakes might prefer a more calculated and strategic approach. Finding a balance in addressing conflicts is crucial for maintaining harmony.

Independence: Both Dragons and Snakes value their independence. Respecting each other's need for freedom and autonomy is important for a healthy relationship.

Risk-Taking: Dragons may be more inclined to take risks, while Snakes tend to be cautious. Balancing these different risk preferences is essential for making important decisions together.

In summary, a marriage between a Dragon and a Snake can have a blend of shared ambition, charisma, and adaptability. Effective communication, understanding and respecting each other's differences, and finding a balance between assertiveness and diplomacy are key to a successful and fulfilling marriage.

Dragon and Horse

Personality Compatibilities

Shared Energy and Enthusiasm: Both Dragons and Horses are known for their energy, enthusiasm, and love for adventure. In a Dragon-Horse relationship, there can be a shared zest for life and a mutual understanding of each other's need for excitement.

Charisma and Magnetism: Dragons and Horses often possess charisma and magnetism. This shared quality can enhance their social interactions and contribute to a dynamic and engaging partnership.

Optimism: Horses are generally optimistic and adventurous, and Dragons are enthusiastic. This shared optimism can create a positive and uplifting atmosphere within the relationship.

Independence: Both Dragons and Horses value their independence. Respecting each other's need for freedom and autonomy is important for a healthy and fulfilling relationship.

Personality Differences

Communication Styles: Dragons may have a more direct and assertive communication style, while Horses are often straightforward and open. Navigating these differences requires mutual understanding and effective communication from both partners.

Handling Conflicts: Dragons may confront conflicts more directly, while Horses might prefer a more spontaneous and direct approach. Finding a balance in addressing conflicts is crucial for maintaining harmony.

Risk-Taking: Both Dragons and Horses can be risk-takers, but Dragons may have a more calculated approach, while Horses might be more impulsive. Balancing these different risk preferences is essential for making important decisions together.

Long-Term Planning: Dragons are often strategic and forward-thinking, while Horses may be more focused on the present. Finding common ground in long-term planning and setting mutual goals is important for the stability of the relationship.

In summary, a marriage between a Dragon and a Horse can have a lively and dynamic energy with shared enthusiasm and optimism. Effective communication, understanding and respecting each other's differences, and finding a balance between spontaneity and strategic planning are key to a successful and fulfilling marriage.

Dragon and Goat

Personality Compatibilities

Shared Appreciation for Beauty: Dragons and Goats may share an appreciation for aesthetics and beauty. This common interest can lead to a harmonious and enriching partnership, especially in the areas of art and culture.

Gentleness: Goats are often gentle and nurturing, and Dragons, despite their intensity, can be understanding. This shared trait can create a nurturing and supportive environment within the relationship.

Creativity: Both Dragons and Goats are associated with artistic and creative interests. Shared hobbies and an interest in creative pursuits can contribute to a fulfilling and dynamic partnership.

Charm: Dragons are known for their charisma, and Goats can be charming in their own way. This shared quality can enhance their social interactions and contribute to a dynamic and engaging relationship.

Personality Differences

Communication Styles: Dragons may have a more direct and assertive communication style, while Goats are often reserved and diplomatic. Navigating these differences requires mutual understanding and effective communication from both partners.

Handling Conflicts: Dragons may confront conflicts more directly, while Goats might prefer a more passive or indirect approach. Finding a balance in addressing conflicts is crucial for maintaining harmony.

Independence: Both Dragons and Goats value their independence, but Dragons may be more assertive in asserting their autonomy. Respecting each other's need for freedom and autonomy is important for a healthy relationship.

Approach to Challenges: Dragons are often strategic and forward-thinking, while Goats may be more introspective and thoughtful. Combining these approaches can lead to a well-rounded problem-solving dynamic.

In summary, a marriage between a Dragon and a Goat can have a blend of shared appreciation for beauty, creativity, and charm. Effective communication, understanding and respecting each other's differences, and finding a balance between assertiveness and diplomacy are key to a successful and fulfilling marriage.

Dragon and Monkey

Personality Compatibilities

Shared Energy and Enthusiasm: Both Dragons and Monkeys are known for their energy, enthusiasm, and love for adventure. In a Dragon-Monkey relationship, there can be a shared zest for life and a mutual understanding of each other's need for excitement.

Charismatic Presence: Dragons and Monkeys often possess charisma and magnetism. This shared quality can enhance their social interactions and contribute to a dynamic and engaging partnership.

Optimism: Monkeys are generally optimistic and resourceful, and Dragons are enthusiastic. This shared optimism can create a positive and uplifting atmosphere within the relationship.

Creativity and Playfulness: Both Dragons and Monkeys can possess creativity and playfulness. Shared interests in artistic pursuits and a love for fun and entertainment can contribute to a dynamic and enjoyable partnership.

Personality Differences

Communication Styles: Dragons may have a more direct and assertive communication style, while Monkeys are communicative and quick-witted. Navigating these differences requires mutual understanding and effective communication from both partners.

Handling Conflicts: Dragons may confront conflicts more directly, while Monkeys might approach issues with a sense of humor and cleverness. Finding a balance in handling conflicts is crucial for maintaining harmony.

Independence: Both Dragons and Monkeys value their independence. Respecting each other's need for freedom and autonomy is important for a healthy and fulfilling relationship.

Approach to Challenges: Dragons are often strategic and forward-thinking, while Monkeys can be adaptable and resourceful. Combining these approaches can lead to a well-rounded problem-solving dynamic.

In summary, a marriage between a Dragon and a Monkey can have a lively and dynamic energy with shared enthusiasm, creativity, and playfulness. Effective communication, understanding and respecting each other's differences, and finding a balance between assertiveness and humor are key to a successful and fulfilling marriage.

Dragon and Rooster

Personality Compatibilities

Balance of Energies: Dragons are known for their energy, charisma, and ambition, while Roosters are practical, diligent, and detail-oriented. In a Dragon-Rooster relationship, there can be a balance where the Dragon's dynamism complements the Rooster's grounded and organized approach.

Charisma and Practicality: Both Dragons and Roosters can possess charisma and practicality. This shared quality can enhance their social interactions and contribute to a dynamic and well-organized partnership.

Ambition: Dragons are ambitious and forward-thinking, and Roosters are diligent and hardworking. This shared ambition can lead to mutual support in pursuing goals and aspirations.

Attention to Detail: Roosters are meticulous and detail-oriented, while Dragons may focus on the bigger picture. Combining these approaches can lead to a well-rounded decision-making process.

Personality Differences

Communication Styles: Dragons may have a more direct and assertive communication style, while Roosters are straightforward and meticulous. Navigating these differences requires mutual understanding and effective communication from both partners.

Handling Conflicts: Dragons may confront conflicts more directly, while Roosters might approach issues with a practical and analytical mindset. Finding a balance in addressing conflicts is crucial for maintaining harmony.

Social Dynamics: Dragons may enjoy a more active and outgoing social life, while Roosters may prefer a smaller, more intimate circle. Finding a compromise in social activities can contribute to a harmonious relationship.

Independence: Both Dragons and Roosters value their independence. Respecting each other's need for freedom and autonomy is important for a healthy relationship.

In summary, a marriage between a Dragon and a Rooster can have a balance of energy, ambition, and practicality. Effective communication, understanding and respecting each other's differences, and finding a balance between assertiveness and attention to detail are key to a successful and fulfilling marriage.

Dragon and Dog

Personality Compatibilities

Loyalty: Both Dragons and Dogs are known for their loyalty and commitment in relationships. This shared value can create a strong bond, fostering trust and mutual support between the partners.

Protectiveness: Dragons, with their strong and dynamic presence, can be protective, and Dogs are naturally protective as well. This shared trait can contribute to a sense of security within the relationship.

Ambition: Dragons are ambitious and forward-thinking, and Dogs are diligent and hardworking. This shared ambition can lead to mutual support in pursuing goals and aspirations.

Harmony: Dogs value harmony and loyalty in relationships, and Dragons, while dynamic, may appreciate stability and commitment. This shared desire for a harmonious partnership can contribute to a positive atmosphere.

Personality Differences

Communication Styles: Dragons may have a more direct and assertive communication style, while Dogs are known for their honesty and straightforwardness. Navigating these differences requires mutual understanding and effective communication from both partners.

Handling Conflicts: Dragons may confront conflicts more directly, while Dogs might approach issues with a sense of loyalty and protectiveness. Finding a balance in addressing conflicts is crucial for maintaining harmony.

Independence: Both Dragons and Dogs value their independence. Respecting each other's need for freedom and autonomy is important for a healthy relationship.

Social Dynamics: Dogs may have a more reserved and cautious approach to socializing, while Dragons may enjoy a more active and outgoing social life. Finding a compromise in social activities can contribute to a harmonious relationship.

In summary, a marriage between a Dragon and a Dog can have a blend of loyalty, protectiveness, and ambition. Effective communication, understanding and respecting each other's differences, and finding a balance between assertiveness and honesty are key to a successful and fulfilling marriage.

Dragon and Pig

Personality Compatibilities

Creativity and Aesthetics: Both Dragons and Pigs are often associated with artistic interests. This shared creativity and appreciation for aesthetics can contribute to a harmonious and enriching partnership, especially in the areas of art and culture.

Gentleness: Pigs are known for their gentle and nurturing nature, and Dragons, despite their intensity, can be understanding. This shared trait can create a nurturing and supportive environment within the relationship.

Optimism: Pigs are generally optimistic and easygoing, and Dragons are enthusiastic. This shared optimism can create a positive and uplifting atmosphere within the relationship.

Charm and Charisma: Dragons are known for their charisma, and Pigs can be charming in their own way. This shared quality can enhance their social interactions and contribute to a dynamic and engaging partnership.

Personality Differences

Communication Styles: Dragons may have a more direct and assertive communication style, while Pigs are often diplomatic and tactful. Navigating these differences requires mutual understanding and effective communication from both partners.

Handling Conflicts: Dragons may confront conflicts more directly, while Pigs might approach issues with a sense of gentleness and compromise. Finding a balance in addressing conflicts is crucial for maintaining harmony.

Independence: Both Dragons and Pigs value their independence. Respecting each other's need for freedom and autonomy is important for a healthy relationship.

Approach to Challenges: Dragons are often strategic and forward-thinking, while Pigs may be more patient and adaptable. Combining these approaches can lead to a well-rounded problem-solving dynamic.

In summary, a marriage between a Dragon and a Pig can have a harmonious blend of creativity, gentleness, and charm. Effective communication, understanding and respecting each other's differences, and finding a balance between assertiveness and compromise are key to a successful and fulfilling marriage.

Snake and Snake

Personality Compatibilities

Emotional Depth: Snakes are known for their emotional depth, intuition, and sensibility. In a Snake-Snake relationship, there can be a shared understanding of each other's feelings and a mutual appreciation for emotional connection.

Charm and Grace: Snakes are often associated with charm, grace, and sophistication. In a Snake-Snake marriage, there can be a shared sense of style and an appreciation for aesthetics.

Privacy: Snakes value their privacy and often prefer a more intimate circle. In a Snake-Snake relationship, there may be a shared understanding of the importance of personal space and privacy.

Strategic Thinking: Snakes are known for their strategic thinking and ability to plan ahead. This shared quality can lead to a well-organized and forward-thinking partnership.

Personality Differences

Communication Styles: While Snakes are generally diplomatic and tactful, they may not always express their emotions openly. Navigating these differences in communication styles requires mutual understanding and openness.

Approach to Challenges: Snakes may be cautious and prefer a thoughtful approach to challenges. In a Snake-Snake marriage, finding a balance between caution and taking necessary risks is essential for navigating obstacles.

Independence: Snakes value their independence, and in a Snake-Snake relationship, respecting each other's need for personal space and autonomy is crucial for a healthy partnership.

Handling Conflicts: Snakes may avoid confrontation to maintain harmony. In a Snake-Snake marriage, finding a constructive way to address conflicts and ensure open communication is important for a strong and enduring relationship.

In summary, a marriage between two Snakes can have a foundation of emotional depth, charm, and strategic thinking. While there are shared traits and values, managing potential challenges related to communication, conflict resolution, and independence is essential for maintaining a healthy and fulfilling relationship.

Snake and Horse

Personality Compatibilities

Balanced Energy: Snakes are often composed, thoughtful, and strategic, while Horses are known for their energy, enthusiasm, and love for adventure. In a Snake-Horse relationship, there can be a balance where the Snake's calmness complements the Horse's dynamism.

Charm and Charisma: Both Snakes and Horses can possess charm and charisma in different ways. This shared quality can enhance their social interactions and contribute to a dynamic and engaging partnership.

Optimism and Pragmatism: Horses are generally optimistic and adventurous, and Snakes are pragmatic and strategic. This combination can lead to a well-rounded approach to both planning for the future and enjoying the present.

Adaptability: Horses are adaptable, and Snakes can be flexible in their thinking. This shared trait can contribute to a relationship that navigates challenges effectively and embraces change when necessary.

Personality Differences

Communication Styles: Snakes may have a more diplomatic and reserved communication style, while Horses are often more straightforward and open. Navigating these differences requires mutual understanding and effective communication from both partners.

Handling Conflicts: Snakes may prefer a more calculated and strategic approach to conflicts, while Horses might be more direct. Finding a balance in addressing conflicts is crucial for maintaining harmony.

Independence: Both Snakes and Horses value their independence. Respecting each other's need for freedom and autonomy is important for a healthy relationship.

Approach to Challenges: Snakes are often strategic and forward-thinking, while Horses can be spontaneous. Combining these approaches can lead to a well-rounded problem-solving dynamic.

In summary, a marriage between a Snake and a Horse can have a balance of energy, charm, and adaptability. Effective communication, understanding and respecting each other's differences, and finding a balance between pragmatism and spontaneity are key to a successful and fulfilling marriage.

Snake and Goat

Personality Compatibilities

Artistic Interests: Both Snakes and Goats are often associated with artistic and creative interests. This shared creativity and appreciation for aesthetics can contribute to a harmonious and enriching partnership, especially in the areas of art and culture.

Gentleness and Compassion: Goats are known for their gentle and compassionate nature, and Snakes, while strategic, can be understanding. This shared trait can create a nurturing and supportive environment within the relationship.

Tactfulness: Snakes are generally diplomatic and tactful, and Goats value harmony. This shared quality can lead to a relationship where conflicts are approached with care and consideration for each other's feelings.

Intuition: Both Snakes and Goats can possess intuition and sensitivity. This shared trait can enhance their emotional connection and understanding of each other's needs.

Personality Differences

Communication Styles: Snakes may have a more reserved communication style, while Goats are often gentle and open. Navigating these differences requires mutual understanding and effective communication from both partners.

Handling Conflicts: Snakes may prefer a more calculated and strategic approach to conflicts, while Goats might approach issues with a desire for peace and compromise. Finding a balance in addressing conflicts is crucial for maintaining harmony.

Independence: Both Snakes and Goats value their independence, but Snakes may be more self-reliant. Respecting each other's need for personal space and autonomy is important for a healthy relationship.

Approach to Challenges: Snakes are often strategic and forward-thinking, while Goats may be more sensitive and introspective. Combining these approaches can lead to a well-rounded problem-solving dynamic.

In summary, a marriage between a Snake and a Goat can have a blend of creativity, gentleness, and compassion. Effective communication, understanding and respecting each other's differences, and finding a balance between tactfulness and strategic thinking are key to a successful and fulfilling marriage.

Snake and Monkey

Personality Compatibilities

Intellectual Compatibility: Both Snakes and Monkeys tend to be intelligent and have a curious nature. This shared intellectual curiosity can lead to engaging conversations and mutual interests in learning and exploring.

Charm and Wit: Snakes are often associated with charm, while Monkeys are known for their wit and cleverness. This shared quality can enhance their social interactions and contribute to a dynamic and engaging partnership.

Adaptability: Monkeys are adaptable and resourceful, and Snakes can be flexible in their thinking. This shared trait can contribute to a relationship that navigates challenges effectively and embraces change when necessary.

Independence: Both Snakes and Monkeys value their independence. Respecting each other's need for freedom and autonomy is important for a healthy relationship.

Personality Differences

Communication Styles: Snakes may have a more reserved and diplomatic communication style, while Monkeys are often more direct and assertive. Navigating these differences requires mutual understanding and effective communication from both partners.

Handling Conflicts: Snakes may prefer a more calculated and strategic approach to conflicts, while Monkeys might be more spontaneous. Finding a balance in addressing conflicts is crucial for maintaining harmony.

Social Dynamics: Monkeys may enjoy a more active and outgoing social life, while Snakes may prefer a smaller, more intimate circle. Finding a compromise in social activities can contribute to a harmonious relationship.

Approach to Challenges: Snakes are often strategic and forward-thinking, while Monkeys can be quick-witted and adaptable. Combining these approaches can lead to a well-rounded problem-solving dynamic.

In summary, a marriage between a Snake and a Monkey can have a mix of intellectual compatibility, charm, and adaptability. Effective communication, understanding and respecting each other's differences, and finding a balance between assertiveness and strategic thinking are key to a successful and fulfilling marriage.

Snake and Rooster

Personality Compatibilities

Strategic Thinking: Snakes are known for their strategic thinking and Roosters are analytical and detail-oriented. In a Snake-Rooster relationship, there can be a shared ability to plan ahead and approach challenges with a thoughtful mindset.

Charm and Precision: Both Snakes and Roosters can possess charm in different ways. This shared quality can enhance their social interactions and contribute to a dynamic and well-organized partnership.

Independence: Both Snakes and Roosters value their independence. Respecting each other's need for freedom and autonomy is important for a healthy relationship.

Diligence: Roosters are diligent and hardworking, and Snakes can be focused and determined. This shared work ethic can lead to a mutual appreciation for each other's commitment to goals and responsibilities.

Personality Differences

Communication Styles: Snakes may have a more reserved communication style, while Roosters are often more straightforward and assertive. Navigating these differences requires mutual understanding and effective communication from both partners.

Handling Conflicts: Snakes may prefer a more calculated and strategic approach to conflicts, while Roosters might be more direct. Finding a balance in addressing conflicts is crucial for maintaining harmony.

Attention to Detail: Roosters are meticulous and detail-oriented, while Snakes may focus on the bigger picture. Combining these approaches can lead to a well-rounded decision-making process.

Social Dynamics: Roosters may enjoy socializing in a more structured and organized manner, while Snakes may prefer a smaller, more intimate circle. Finding a compromise in social activities can contribute to a harmonious relationship.

In summary, a marriage between a Snake and a Rooster can have a balance of strategic thinking, charm, and diligence. Effective communication, understanding and respecting each other's differences, and finding a balance between assertiveness and attention to detail are key to a successful and fulfilling marriage.

Snake and Dog

Personality Compatibilities

Loyalty: Both Snakes and Dogs are known for their loyalty and commitment in relationships. This shared value can create a strong bond, fostering trust and mutual support between the partners.

Protectiveness: Dogs are naturally protective, and Snakes, with their strong and strategic nature, can be protective as well. This shared trait can contribute to a sense of security within the relationship.

Independence: Both Snakes and Dogs value their independence. Respecting each other's need for freedom and autonomy is important for a healthy relationship.

Intuition: Snakes are often intuitive, and Dogs are known for their keen sense of intuition and loyalty. This shared trait can enhance their emotional connection and understanding of each other's needs.

Personality Differences

Communication Styles: Snakes may have a more reserved and diplomatic communication style, while Dogs are honest and straightforward. Navigating these differences requires mutual understanding and effective communication from both partners.

Handling Conflicts: Snakes may prefer a more calculated and strategic approach to conflicts, while Dogs might be more direct. Finding a balance in addressing conflicts is crucial for maintaining harmony.

Approach to Challenges: Snakes are often strategic and forward-thinking, while Dogs can be practical and down-to-earth. Combining these approaches can lead to a well-rounded problem-solving dynamic.

Social Dynamics: Dogs may enjoy socializing and connecting with others, while Snakes may prefer a smaller, more intimate circle. Finding a compromise in social activities can contribute to a harmonious relationship.

In summary, a marriage between a Snake and a Dog can have a foundation of loyalty, protectiveness, and independence. Effective communication, understanding and respecting each other's differences, and finding a balance between assertiveness and practicality are key to a successful and fulfilling marriage.

Snake and Pig

Personality Compatibilities

Diplomacy: Both Snakes and Pigs can be diplomatic and tactful in their interactions. This shared quality can contribute to a harmonious and understanding relationship.

Intuition: Snakes are often intuitive, and Pigs are known for their keen perception. This shared trait can enhance their emotional connection and understanding of each other's feelings.

Charm: Snakes are associated with charm, and Pigs can be charming in their own way. This shared quality can contribute to a pleasant and engaging partnership.

Calmness: Pigs are generally calm and easygoing, and Snakes, while strategic, can be composed. This shared trait can create a peaceful and balanced atmosphere within the relationship.

Personality Differences

Communication Styles: Snakes may have a more reserved and diplomatic communication style, while Pigs are often more open and trusting. Navigating these differences requires mutual understanding and effective communication from both partners.

Handling Conflicts: Snakes may prefer a more calculated and strategic approach to conflicts, while Pigs might be more inclined to seek harmony through compromise. Finding a balance in addressing conflicts is crucial for maintaining harmony.

Approach to Challenges: Snakes are often strategic and forward-thinking, while Pigs may be more patient and adaptable. Combining these approaches can lead to a well-rounded problem-solving dynamic.

Independence: Both Snakes and Pigs value their independence, but Snakes may be more self-reliant. Respecting each other's need for personal space and autonomy is important for a healthy relationship.

In summary, a marriage between a Snake and a Pig can have a blend of diplomacy, charm, and calmness. Effective communication, understanding and respecting each other's differences, and finding a balance between assertiveness and compromise are key to a successful and fulfilling marriage.

Horse and Horse

Personality Compatibilities

Energy and Enthusiasm: Horses are known for their energy, enthusiasm, and love for adventure. In a Horse-Horse relationship, there can be a shared zest for life and mutual interest in exploring new experiences and activities.

Optimism: Horses are generally optimistic, and in a Horse-Horse marriage, this shared positive outlook can contribute to a lively and uplifting atmosphere within the relationship.

Independence: Horses value their independence, and in a Horse-Horse relationship, there can be mutual respect for each other's need for personal freedom and space.

Sense of Adventure: Both individuals may share a love for spontaneity and a sense of adventure, making their relationship dynamic and exciting.

Personality Differences

Communication Styles: Horses may be straightforward and direct in their communication. Navigating these similarities requires effective communication to ensure mutual understanding.

Handling Conflicts: Horses may confront conflicts directly, and in a Horse-Horse marriage, finding a constructive way to address issues and maintain harmony is crucial.

Attention Span: Horses can be known for their restless nature and occasional impatience. Both partners may need to find activities and interests that hold their attention for a lasting and fulfilling relationship.

Commitment: While Horses can be deeply committed, they may also value their independence. Balancing individual freedom with commitment to the relationship is essential.

In summary, a marriage between two Horses can have a high level of energy, enthusiasm, and a shared sense of adventure. Effective communication, understanding and respecting each other's need for independence, and finding ways to keep the relationship engaging and committed are key to a successful and fulfilling marriage.

Horse and Goat

Personality Compatibilities

Charm: Both Horses and Goats can possess charm in different ways. This shared quality can enhance their social interactions and contribute to a pleasant and engaging partnership.

Creativity: Goats are often associated with artistic and creative interests, and Horses can appreciate variety and excitement. This shared creativity can lead to a harmonious and enriching relationship, especially in the areas of art and culture.

Optimism: Horses are generally optimistic, and Goats are gentle and easygoing. This shared positive outlook can contribute to a lighthearted and positive atmosphere within the relationship.

Adaptability: Goats are adaptable, and Horses are known for their love of adventure. This shared trait can contribute to a relationship that navigates changes and challenges effectively.

Personality Differences

Communication Styles: Horses may be more straightforward and direct in their communication, while Goats may be more reserved. Navigating these differences requires mutual understanding and effective communication from both partners.

Handling Conflicts: Horses may confront conflicts more directly, while Goats might approach issues with a desire for peace and compromise. Finding a balance in addressing conflicts is crucial for maintaining harmony.

Approach to Challenges: Horses can be spontaneous, while Goats may be more patient and introspective. Combining these approaches can lead to a well-rounded problem-solving dynamic.

Independence: Both Horses and Goats value their independence. Respecting each other's need for personal space and autonomy is important for a healthy relationship.

In summary, a marriage between a Horse and a Goat can have a blend of charm, creativity, and adaptability. Effective communication, understanding and respecting each other's differences, and finding a balance between assertiveness and compromise are key to a successful and fulfilling marriage.

Horse and Monkey

Personality Compatibilities

Energy and Enthusiasm: Horses are known for their energy and love for adventure, and Monkeys are lively and energetic. In a Horse-Monkey relationship, there can be a shared zest for life and mutual interest in exploring new experiences and activities.

Sense of Humor: Monkeys are known for their wit and sense of humor, and Horses can appreciate lightheartedness. This shared quality can contribute to a relationship that is dynamic and enjoyable.

Optimism: Horses are generally optimistic, and Monkeys are quick-witted and adaptable. This shared positive outlook can contribute to a lively and uplifting atmosphere within the relationship.

Independence: Both Horses and Monkeys value their independence. Respecting each other's need for personal freedom and space is important for a healthy relationship.

Personality Differences

Communication Styles: Horses may be more straightforward and direct in their communication, while Monkeys are often quick-witted and humorous. Navigating these differences requires mutual understanding and effective communication from both partners.

Handling Conflicts: Horses may confront conflicts more directly, while Monkeys might use humor and creativity to diffuse tension. Finding a balance in addressing conflicts is crucial for maintaining harmony.

Attention Span: Monkeys can be curious and easily distracted, while Horses may seek continuous excitement. Both partners may need to find activities and interests that keep them engaged and fulfilled.

Approach to Challenges: Horses can be spontaneous, while Monkeys are adaptable and resourceful. Combining these approaches can lead to a well-rounded problem-solving dynamic.

In summary, a marriage between a Horse and a Monkey can have a high level of energy, enthusiasm, and a shared sense of humor. Effective communication, understanding and respecting each other's differences, and finding ways to keep the relationship engaging and dynamic are key to a successful and fulfilling marriage.

Horse and Rooster

Personality Compatibilities

Hard Work and Ambition: Both Horses and Roosters can be ambitious and hardworking. This shared trait can contribute to a mutual drive for success and accomplishment within the relationship.

Optimism: Horses are generally optimistic, and Roosters are practical and realistic. This combination can provide a balanced perspective on both goals and challenges, contributing to a well-rounded partnership.

Independence: Both Horses and Roosters value their independence. Respecting each other's need for personal freedom and autonomy is important for a healthy relationship.

Energy: Horses are known for their energy, and Roosters are active and energetic. This shared dynamism can contribute to a relationship that is lively and engaging.

Personality Differences

Communication Styles: Horses may be more straightforward and direct in their communication, while Roosters are often more detail-oriented and assertive. Navigating these differences requires mutual understanding and effective communication from both partners.

Handling Conflicts: Horses may confront conflicts more directly, while Roosters might approach issues with a sense of practicality. Finding a balance in addressing conflicts is crucial for maintaining harmony.

Approach to Challenges: Horses can be spontaneous, while Roosters are strategic and forward-thinking. Combining these approaches can lead to a well-rounded problem-solving dynamic.

Social Dynamics: Roosters may prefer structured social interactions, while Horses may enjoy a more spontaneous and varied social life. Finding a compromise in social activities can contribute to a harmonious relationship.

In summary, a marriage between a Horse and a Rooster can have a blend of ambition, optimism, and energy. Effective communication, understanding and respecting each other's differences, and finding a balance between assertiveness and practicality are key to a successful and fulfilling marriage.

Horse and Dog

Personality Compatibilities

Loyalty: Both Horses and Dogs are known for their loyalty and commitment in relationships. This shared value can create a strong bond, fostering trust and mutual support between the partners.

Energy: Horses are known for their energy, and Dogs are active and energetic as well. This shared dynamism can contribute to a relationship that is lively and engaging.

Optimism: Horses are generally optimistic, and Dogs are known for their honesty and straightforwardness. This combination can provide a balanced perspective on both positive outlooks and realistic assessments.

Independence: Both Horses and Dogs value their independence. Respecting each other's need for personal freedom and space is important for a healthy relationship.

Personality Differences

Communication Styles: Horses may be more straightforward and direct in their communication, while Dogs are known for their honesty and loyalty. Navigating these differences requires mutual understanding and effective communication from both partners.

Handling Conflicts: Horses may confront conflicts more directly, while Dogs might approach issues with a sense of loyalty and protective instincts. Finding a balance in addressing conflicts is crucial for maintaining harmony.

Approach to Challenges: Horses can be spontaneous, while Dogs are diligent and practical. Combining these approaches can lead to a well-rounded problem-solving dynamic.

Social Dynamics: Dogs may enjoy socializing in a more structured and loyal manner, while Horses may prefer a more spontaneous and varied social life. Finding a compromise in social activities can contribute to a harmonious relationship.

In summary, a marriage between a Horse and a Dog can have a blend of loyalty, energy, and optimism. Effective communication, understanding and respecting each other's differences, and finding a balance between assertiveness and practicality are key to a successful and fulfilling marriage.

Horse and Pig

Personality Compatibilities

Optimism: Both Horses and Pigs are generally optimistic. This shared positive outlook can contribute to a relationship that is uplifting and enjoyable.

Independence: Both Horses and Pigs value their independence. Respecting each other's need for personal freedom and space is important for a healthy relationship.

Charm: Horses are associated with charm, and Pigs can be charming in their own way. This shared quality can enhance their social interactions and contribute to a pleasant and engaging partnership.

Energy: Horses are known for their energy, and Pigs, while generally calm, can appreciate and match the dynamic nature of Horses, creating a lively relationship.

Personality Differences

Communication Styles: Horses may be more straightforward and direct in their communication, while Pigs may approach communication with a more gentle and considerate manner. Navigating these differences requires mutual understanding and effective communication from both partners.

Handling Conflicts: Horses may confront conflicts more directly, while Pigs might approach issues with a desire for peace and compromise. Finding a balance in addressing conflicts is crucial for maintaining harmony.

Approach to Challenges: Horses can be spontaneous, while Pigs may be more patient and practical. Combining these approaches can lead to a well-rounded problem-solving dynamic.

Social Dynamics: Pigs may enjoy socializing in a more easygoing and sociable manner, while Horses may prefer a more spontaneous and varied social life. Finding a compromise in social activities can contribute to a harmonious relationship.

In summary, a marriage between a Horse and a Pig can have a blend of optimism, charm, and energy. Effective communication, understanding and respecting each other's differences, and finding a balance between assertiveness and compromise are key to a successful and fulfilling marriage.

Goat and Goat

Personality Compatibilities

Sensitivity: Goats are known for their sensitivity and empathy. In a Goat-Goat relationship, there can be a shared understanding of each other's emotional needs, fostering a supportive and compassionate connection.

Creativity: Goats are often associated with artistic and creative pursuits. In a Goat-Goat marriage, there can be shared interests in artistic endeavors, leading to a harmonious and enriching partnership.

Gentleness: Goats are generally gentle and peace-loving. A Goat-Goat relationship may benefit from the mutual desire for a tranquil and harmonious home environment.

Caring Nature: Goats are caring and nurturing. In a Goat-Goat relationship, there can be a natural inclination to care for each other, creating a loving and supportive atmosphere.

Personality Differences

Communication Styles: Goats may be more reserved in their communication. In a Goat-Goat marriage, both partners may need to encourage open communication to avoid misunderstandings.

Handling Conflicts: Goats may avoid confrontations, and in a Goat-Goat relationship, finding constructive ways to address issues is important for maintaining harmony.

Decision-Making: Goats may struggle with decision-making, and in a Goat-Goat marriage, both partners may need to work together to make decisions, ensuring a balanced and decisive approach.

Independence: While Goats value their independence, in a Goat-Goat relationship, there may be a need for both partners to find a balance between individual freedom and shared responsibilities.

In summary, a marriage between two Goats can have a foundation of sensitivity, creativity, and a caring nature. Effective communication, understanding and respecting each other's differences, and finding a balance between assertiveness and compromise are key to a successful and fulfilling marriage.

Goat and Monkey

Personality Compatibilities

Playfulness: Both Goats and Monkeys can be playful and enjoy a sense of fun and spontaneity. This shared quality can contribute to a relationship that is lively and entertaining.

Charm: Goats are associated with charm, and Monkeys are clever and charming in their own way. This shared quality can enhance their social interactions and contribute to a pleasant and engaging partnership.

Adaptability: Monkeys are known for their adaptability, and Goats, while generally gentle, can appreciate the Monkey's ability to navigate various situations. This shared trait can contribute to a dynamic and flexible relationship.

Creativity: Goats are often associated with artistic pursuits, and Monkeys are known for their creativity and cleverness. This shared interest can lead to a harmonious and enriching partnership, especially in the realm of artistic endeavors.

Personality Differences

Communication Styles: Monkeys may be more outgoing and direct in their communication, while Goats may be more reserved. Navigating these differences requires mutual understanding and effective communication from both partners.

Handling Conflicts: Monkeys may confront conflicts more directly, while Goats might approach issues with a desire for peace and compromise. Finding a balance in addressing conflicts is crucial for maintaining harmony.

Attention Span: Monkeys can be curious and easily distracted, while Goats may have a more patient and introspective nature. Both partners may need to find activities and interests that hold their attention for a lasting and fulfilling relationship.

Approach to Challenges: Goats may appreciate a more steady and cautious approach, while Monkeys are often more adventurous and spontaneous. Balancing these approaches can lead to a well-rounded problem-solving dynamic.

In summary, a marriage between a Goat and a Monkey can have a blend of playfulness, charm, and adaptability. Effective communication, understanding and respecting each other's differences, and finding a balance between spontaneity and patience are key to a successful and fulfilling marriage.

Goat and Rooster

Personality Compatibilities

Gentleness and Sensitivity: Goats are generally gentle and sensitive, and in a Goat-Rooster relationship, the Rooster's practicality may balance the Goat's emotional nature. This can create a harmonious and understanding dynamic.

Hard Work: Roosters are known for their hard work and attention to detail, and Goats, while more laid-back, can appreciate and benefit from the Rooster's industrious nature. This shared commitment to tasks can contribute to a balanced partnership.

Charm: Both Goats and Roosters can possess charm in different ways. This shared quality can enhance their social interactions and contribute to a pleasant and engaging partnership.

Creativity: Goats are often associated with artistic pursuits, and Roosters can be creative in their own right. This shared interest can lead to a harmonious and enriching partnership, especially in creative endeavors.

Personality Differences

Communication Styles: Roosters tend to be more direct and critical in their communication, while Goats may be more reserved and diplomatic. Navigating these differences requires mutual understanding and effective communication from both partners.

Handling Conflicts: Roosters may confront conflicts directly, while Goats might approach issues with a desire for peace and compromise. Finding a balance in addressing conflicts is crucial for maintaining harmony.

Approach to Challenges: Roosters are practical and strategic, while Goats may appreciate a more steady and cautious approach. Combining these approaches can lead to a well-rounded problem-solving dynamic.

Social Dynamics: Goats may enjoy socializing in a more easygoing and sociable manner, while Roosters may prefer structured social interactions. Finding a compromise in social activities can contribute to a harmonious relationship.

In summary, a marriage between a Goat and a Rooster can have a blend of gentleness, hard work, and charm. Effective communication, understanding and respecting each other's differences, and finding a balance between directness and diplomacy are key to a successful and fulfilling marriage.

Goat and Dog

Personality Compatibilities

Loyalty: Both Goats and Dogs are known for their loyalty in relationships. This shared value can create a strong bond, fostering trust and mutual support between the partners.

Sensitivity: Goats are generally sensitive, and Dogs are emotionally attuned and protective. This shared trait can contribute to a relationship that is understanding and supportive of each other's feelings.

Gentleness: Goats are gentle and easygoing, and Dogs are protective with a gentle nature. This shared gentleness can create a peaceful and harmonious atmosphere within the relationship.

Compassion: Both Goats and Dogs are compassionate individuals. This shared quality can contribute to a relationship where both partners care deeply for each other's well-being.

Personality Differences

Communication Styles: Dogs are known for their straightforward communication, while Goats may be more reserved. Navigating these differences requires mutual understanding and effective communication from both partners.

Handling Conflicts: Dogs may confront conflicts directly, while Goats might approach issues with a desire for peace and compromise. Finding a balance in addressing conflicts is crucial for maintaining harmony.

Independence: Both Goats and Dogs value their independence. Respecting each other's need for personal freedom and space is important for a healthy relationship.

Approach to Challenges: Dogs are diligent and protective, while Goats may appreciate a more laid-back and patient approach. Combining these approaches can lead to a well-rounded problem-solving dynamic.

In summary, a marriage between a Goat and a Dog can have a foundation of loyalty, sensitivity, and compassion. Effective communication, understanding and respecting each other's differences, and finding a balance between assertiveness and compromise are key to a successful and fulfilling marriage.

Goat and Pig

Personality Compatibilities

Gentleness and Harmony: Both Goats and Pigs are known for their gentle and harmonious nature. This shared quality can contribute to a relationship that is peaceful and understanding, fostering a tranquil atmosphere.

Sensitivity: Goats are generally sensitive, and Pigs are empathetic. This shared trait can create a strong emotional connection, as both partners are likely to be attuned to each other's feelings.

Creativity: Goats are often associated with artistic pursuits, and Pigs can appreciate and participate in creative endeavors. This shared interest can lead to a harmonious and enriching partnership.

Adaptability: Pigs are adaptable, and while Goats may prefer stability, their willingness to adapt can contribute to a relationship that navigates changes effectively.

Personality Differences

Communication Styles: Pigs may be more diplomatic and reserved in their communication, while Goats can sometimes be indecisive. Navigating these differences requires mutual understanding and effective communication from both partners.

Handling Conflicts: Pigs may approach conflicts with a desire for peace and compromise, while Goats might avoid confrontations. Finding a balance in addressing conflicts is crucial for maintaining harmony.

Approach to Challenges: Pigs are diligent and hardworking, and Goats may appreciate this dedication. Combining these approaches can lead to a well-rounded problem-solving dynamic.

Independence: Both Goats and Pigs value their independence. Respecting each other's need for personal freedom and space is important for a healthy relationship.

In summary, a marriage between a Goat and a Pig can have a foundation of gentleness, sensitivity, and creativity. Effective communication, understanding and respecting each other's differences, and finding a balance between adaptability and stability are key to a successful and fulfilling marriage.

Monkey and Monkey

Personality Compatibilities

Playfulness and Humor: Monkeys are known for their playfulness and sense of humor. In a Monkey-Monkey relationship, there can be a shared enjoyment of fun activities and a mutual understanding of each other's sense of humor.

Adaptability: Monkeys are adaptable and quick-witted. In a Monkey-Monkey marriage, both partners may find it easy to adapt to changing circumstances and share a dynamic approach to life.

Intelligence: Monkeys are generally intelligent and resourceful. In a Monkey-Monkey relationship, there can be a mutual appreciation for each other's cleverness and intellectual pursuits.

Charm: Monkeys are charming, and in a Monkey-Monkey marriage, this shared quality can enhance their social interactions, making them a socially engaging couple.

Personality Differences

Competitiveness: Monkeys can be competitive, and in a Monkey-Monkey relationship, finding a balance in competitiveness is important to avoid conflicts. Collaborating rather than competing can strengthen the partnership.

Restlessness: Monkeys may have a restless nature, and in a Monkey-Monkey marriage, both partners may need to find constructive ways to channel their energy to prevent boredom or dissatisfaction.

Attention Span: Monkeys can be easily distracted, and in a Monkey-Monkey relationship, finding activities that keep both partners engaged and satisfied is crucial for a lasting and fulfilling connection.

Communication Styles: While Monkeys are generally expressive, they may sometimes have different communication styles. Ensuring open communication and understanding each other's needs is essential for maintaining a strong connection.

In summary, a marriage between two Monkeys can have a foundation of playfulness, adaptability, and intelligence. Effective communication, understanding and respecting each other's differences, and finding ways to channel their energy constructively are key to a successful and fulfilling marriage.

Monkey and Rooster

Personality Compatibilities

Creativity: Both Monkeys and Roosters can be creative in their own ways. This shared interest can lead to a dynamic and enriching partnership, especially in artistic endeavors or problem-solving.

Resourcefulness: Monkeys are known for their resourcefulness, and Roosters are diligent and detail-oriented. This combination can result in a well-rounded approach to tasks and challenges, enhancing their efficiency as a couple.

Optimism: Monkeys are generally optimistic, and Roosters are practical and realistic. This combination can provide a balanced perspective on both positive outlooks and realistic assessments.

Communication Styles: While there may be differences, both Monkeys and Roosters value effective communication. Finding common ground and being open to each other's communication styles can contribute to a healthy relationship.

Personality Differences

Handling Conflicts: Monkeys may prefer a more laid-back and humorous approach to conflicts, while Roosters may be more direct and assertive. Navigating these differences requires mutual understanding and compromise.

Attention to Detail: Roosters are detail-oriented, while Monkeys may be more inclined to focus on the bigger picture. Finding a balance between attention to detail and a broader perspective is essential for harmony.

Independence: Both Monkeys and Roosters value their independence. Respecting each other's need for personal freedom and space is important for a healthy relationship.

Social Dynamics: Monkeys may enjoy socializing in a more playful and spontaneous manner, while Roosters may prefer structured social interactions. Finding a compromise in social activities can contribute to a harmonious relationship.

In summary, a marriage between a Monkey and a Rooster can have a blend of creativity, resourcefulness, and optimism. Effective communication, understanding and respecting each other's differences, and finding a balance between playfulness and practicality are key to a successful and fulfilling marriage.

Monkey and Dog

Personality Compatibilities

Playfulness: Both Monkeys and Dogs can be playful and enjoy a sense of fun and spontaneity. This shared quality can contribute to a relationship that is lively and entertaining.

Loyalty: Dogs are known for their loyalty, and Monkeys, while more independent, can appreciate and reciprocate loyalty. This shared value can create a strong bond and sense of security in the relationship.

Optimism: Monkeys are generally optimistic, and Dogs are sincere and straightforward. This combination can provide a balanced perspective on both positive outlooks and realistic assessments.

Resourcefulness: Monkeys are known for their resourcefulness, and Dogs are diligent and protective. This combination can result in a well-rounded approach to tasks and challenges, enhancing their efficiency as a couple.

Personality Differences

Communication Styles: Monkeys may be more outgoing and direct in their communication, while Dogs may be more reserved. Navigating these differences requires mutual understanding and effective communication from both partners.

Handling Conflicts: Monkeys may prefer a more laid-back and humorous approach to conflicts, while Dogs may be more serious and protective. Finding a balance in addressing conflicts is crucial for maintaining harmony.

Attention to Detail: Dogs are detail-oriented, while Monkeys may be more inclined to focus on the bigger picture. Finding a balance between attention to detail and a broader perspective is essential for harmony.

Independence: Both Monkeys and Dogs value their independence. Respecting each other's need for personal freedom and space is important for a healthy relationship.

In summary, a marriage between a Monkey and a Dog can have a blend of playfulness, loyalty, and optimism. Effective communication, understanding and respecting each other's differences, and finding a balance between outgoingness and reserve are key to a successful and fulfilling marriage.

Monkey and Pig

Personality Compatibilities

Playfulness: Both Monkeys and Pigs can be playful and enjoy a sense of fun and spontaneity. This shared quality can contribute to a relationship that is lively and entertaining.

Creativity: Monkeys are often associated with artistic pursuits, and Pigs can appreciate and participate in creative endeavors. This shared interest can lead to a harmonious and enriching partnership.

Optimism: Monkeys are generally optimistic, and Pigs are known for their positivity and generosity. This combination can provide a balanced perspective on both positive outlooks and realistic assessments.

Adaptability: Monkeys are adaptable, and Pigs are easygoing. This shared trait can contribute to a relationship that navigates changes effectively and maintains a harmonious atmosphere.

Personality Differences

Communication Styles: Monkeys may be more outgoing and direct in their communication, while Pigs may be more diplomatic and reserved. Navigating these differences requires mutual understanding and effective communication from both partners.

Handling Conflicts: Monkeys may prefer a more laid-back and humorous approach to conflicts, while Pigs may avoid confrontations. Finding a balance in addressing conflicts is crucial for maintaining harmony.

Attention to Detail: Pigs are generally detail-oriented, while Monkeys may be more inclined to focus on the bigger picture. Finding a balance between attention to detail and a broader perspective is essential for harmony.

Independence: Both Monkeys and Pigs value their independence. Respecting each other's need for personal freedom and space is important for a healthy relationship.

In summary, a marriage between a Monkey and a Pig can have a blend of playfulness, creativity, and optimism. Effective communication, understanding and respecting each other's differences, and finding a balance between outgoingness and diplomacy are key to a successful and fulfilling marriage.

Rooster and Rooster

Personality Compatibilities

Hard Work Ethic: Roosters are known for their diligence and hard work. In a Rooster-Rooster relationship, there can be a shared commitment to achieving goals and maintaining a strong work ethic.

Practicality: Roosters are practical and detail-oriented. This shared quality can contribute to a well-organized and efficient partnership, especially when it comes to managing daily tasks and responsibilities.

Honesty: Roosters value honesty, and in a Rooster-Rooster marriage, there can be an expectation of open and straightforward communication, fostering trust between the partners.

Resourcefulness: Roosters are resourceful problem solvers. In a Rooster-Rooster relationship, this shared ability can lead to effective solutions when faced with challenges.

Personality Differences

Competitiveness: Roosters can be competitive, and in a Rooster-Rooster relationship, finding a balance in competitiveness is important to avoid conflicts. Collaborating rather than competing can strengthen the partnership.

Critical Nature: Roosters can be critical, and in a Rooster-Rooster marriage, it's essential to balance constructive criticism with positive reinforcement to maintain a supportive atmosphere.

Attention to Detail: Roosters are detail-oriented, and while this can contribute to precision, there may be a need to balance this with a broader perspective to avoid becoming overly focused on minor details.

Independence: Roosters value their independence. In a Rooster-Rooster relationship, it's important for both partners to respect each other's need for personal freedom and space.

In summary, a marriage between two Roosters can have a foundation of hard work, practicality, and honesty. Effective communication, understanding and respecting each other's differences, and finding a balance between competitiveness and collaboration are key to a successful and fulfilling marriage.

Rooster and Dog

Personality Compatibilities

Honesty: Both Roosters and Dogs value honesty and integrity. This shared commitment to truthfulness can create a foundation of trust within the relationship.

Loyalty: Dogs are known for their loyalty, and Roosters appreciate loyalty in their relationships. This shared value can lead to a strong and supportive bond between the partners.

Practicality: Roosters are practical and detail-oriented, and Dogs are pragmatic. This shared practicality can contribute to a well-organized and efficient partnership, especially in managing daily responsibilities.

Commitment to Work: Roosters are hardworking, and Dogs are diligent and dedicated. This shared commitment to work and responsibility can lead to a strong work ethic within the relationship.

Personality Differences

Communication Styles: Roosters can be more critical and direct in their communication, while Dogs may be more sensitive. Navigating these differences requires mutual understanding and finding a balance in expressing opinions.

Approach to Challenges: Roosters are strategic and analytical, while Dogs may approach challenges with a more emotional and empathetic mindset. Combining these approaches can lead to a well-rounded problem-solving dynamic.

Social Dynamics: Roosters can be social but may have a more formal demeanor, while Dogs are generally friendly and approachable. Finding a balance in social interactions can contribute to a harmonious relationship.

Independence: Both Roosters and Dogs value their independence. Respecting each other's need for personal freedom and space is important for a healthy relationship.

In summary, a marriage between a Rooster and a Dog can have a foundation of honesty, loyalty, and practicality. Effective communication, understanding and respecting each other's differences, and finding a balance between directness and sensitivity are key to a successful and fulfilling marriage.

Rooster and Pig

Personality Compatibilities

Hard Work Ethic: Both Roosters and Pigs can be hardworking and diligent. This shared quality can contribute to a strong commitment to achieving shared goals and maintaining a stable lifestyle.

Resourcefulness: Roosters are known for their resourcefulness, and Pigs are generally adaptable. This combination can lead to effective problem-solving and a dynamic approach to challenges.

Loyalty: Pigs are loyal, and Roosters appreciate loyalty in relationships. This shared value can create a strong bond and sense of security within the marriage.

Attention to Detail: Roosters are detail-oriented, and Pigs, while generally easygoing, can appreciate the precision and organization that Roosters bring. This combination can lead to a well-organized and efficient partnership.

Personality Differences

Communication Styles: Roosters can be more critical and direct in their communication, while Pigs may prefer a more diplomatic and gentle approach. Navigating these differences requires mutual understanding and finding a balance in expressing opinions.

Handling Conflicts: Roosters may confront conflicts directly, while Pigs may avoid confrontations. Finding a balance in addressing conflicts is crucial for maintaining harmony.

Optimism: Pigs are generally optimistic, and Roosters are pragmatic. Balancing realistic assessments with positivity is important for maintaining a balanced perspective on life.

Independence: Both Roosters and Pigs value their independence. Respecting each other's need for personal freedom and space is important for a healthy relationship.

In summary, a marriage between a Rooster and a Pig can have a foundation of hard work, loyalty, and resourcefulness. Effective communication, understanding and respecting each other's differences, and finding a balance between directness and diplomacy are key to a successful and fulfilling marriage.

Dog and Dog

Personality Compatibilities

Loyalty: Dogs are known for their loyalty, and in a Dog-Dog relationship, there can be a deep and mutual commitment to each other. Loyalty can create a strong foundation for trust and support.

Honesty: Dogs value honesty and sincerity. In a Dog-Dog marriage, open and straightforward communication may be a strong suit, contributing to a relationship built on trust and transparency.

Compassion: Dogs are compassionate by nature, and in a Dog-Dog relationship, both partners may have a strong sense of empathy and concern for each other's well-being.

Work Ethic: Dogs are diligent and hardworking. In a Dog-Dog marriage, there can be shared values regarding responsibility and a strong work ethic, contributing to a stable and secure partnership.

Personality Differences

Communication Styles: While Dogs value honesty, they may also be reserved in their communication. In a Dog-Dog relationship, navigating potential communication barriers and ensuring open dialogue is crucial.

Handling Conflicts: Dogs may avoid confrontations, seeking harmony in relationships. In a Dog-Dog marriage, addressing conflicts in a constructive manner without avoiding important discussions is essential for growth.

Independence: Dogs value their independence. In a Dog-Dog relationship, respecting each other's need for personal freedom and space is important for maintaining a healthy and balanced partnership.

Worry and Anxiety: Dogs are known for their tendency to worry and be anxious. In a Dog-Dog marriage, finding ways to support each other through moments of stress and providing reassurance can enhance the relationship.

In summary, a marriage between two Dogs can have a strong foundation of loyalty, honesty, and compassion. Effective communication, understanding and respecting each other's differences, and finding a balance between independence and togetherness are key to a successful and fulfilling marriage.

Dog and Pig

Personality Compatibilities

Loyalty: Both Dogs and Pigs are known for their loyalty. This shared value can create a strong sense of commitment and trust within the relationship.

Compassion: Dogs are compassionate, and Pigs are generally kind and gentle. This shared trait can contribute to a relationship that is empathetic and understanding of each other's feelings.

Harmony-Seeking: Both Dogs and Pigs tend to seek harmony in their relationships. This shared desire for a peaceful and stable environment can lead to a supportive and cooperative partnership.

Social Nature: Pigs are sociable, and Dogs, while more reserved, appreciate social connections. This combination can lead to a well-balanced social life as a couple.

Personality Differences

Communication Styles: Dogs may be more reserved in their communication, while Pigs are generally more diplomatic. Navigating these differences requires mutual understanding and finding a balance in expressing opinions.

Worry and Anxiety: Dogs are known for their tendency to worry and be anxious, while Pigs are often more laid-back. Finding ways to alleviate stress and provide reassurance is important for maintaining emotional well-being.

Independence: Both Dogs and Pigs value their independence, but Dogs may have a more protective and vigilant nature. Respecting each other's need for personal freedom and space is crucial for a healthy relationship.

Financial Perspectives: Dogs may be more cautious with finances, while Pigs may enjoy indulging in life's pleasures. Finding a balance in financial decisions and priorities is important for a harmonious partnership.

In summary, a marriage between a Dog and a Pig can have a foundation of loyalty, compassion, and a shared desire for harmony. Effective communication, understanding and respecting each other's differences, and finding a balance between reserve and diplomacy are key to a successful and fulfilling marriage.

Pig and Pig

Personality Compatibilities

Kindness and Generosity: Both Pigs are inherently kind-hearted and compassionate, creating a nurturing and supportive environment within their relationship.

Gentleness and Harmony: Pigs value peace and harmony in their surroundings, leading to a harmonious and loving partnership where conflicts are resolved with empathy and understanding.

Emotional Connection: With their sensitive and intuitive nature, Pig partners share a deep emotional bond, intuitively understanding each other's needs and providing unwavering support.

Enjoyment of Pleasures: Pigs appreciate the finer things in life and take pleasure in simple joys, leading to shared experiences of indulging in good food, relaxation, and leisure activities together.

Personality Differences

Indecisiveness: Pigs may struggle with decision-making, as both partners tend to be indecisive or overly trusting, which can lead to difficulties in taking initiative or making important choices.

Avoidance of Confrontation: Pigs avoid conflict and may be hesitant to address issues directly, leading to unresolved tensions or passive-aggressive behavior if concerns are not openly communicated and addressed.

Over-reliance on Others: While Pigs are generous and supportive, there's a risk of becoming overly dependent on each other for emotional validation or practical support, potentially hindering individual growth and self-reliance.

Financial Management: Pigs may share a tendency to be extravagant or overly indulgent, which can lead to financial challenges if both partners struggle with budgeting or saving money effectively.

Overall, a relationship between two Pig individuals is characterized by warmth, affection, and a deep emotional connection. However, addressing potential conflicts requires open communication, proactive decision-making, and a willingness to find balance between mutual support and individual autonomy.

Afterword

The practice of using astrological and zodiac representations to analyze relationships has a rich history that spans various cultures. While the Chinese zodiac is one tradition, Western astrology has also played a significant role in examining compatibility between individuals.

In Western astrology, the study of how the positions of celestial bodies at the time of one's birth can influence personality and relationships has been a longstanding tradition. Astrologers analyze birth charts, considering the positions of the sun, moon, planets, and other celestial bodies to provide insights into an individual's character and potential compatibility with others.

Similarly, in Chinese culture, the Chinese zodiac assigns each person a specific animal sign based on their birth year, providing a framework for understanding personality traits, strengths, and potential challenges. The compatibility between different zodiac signs has been explored for centuries, offering guidance on how individuals with specific animal signs may interact harmoniously or face challenges in relationships.

While these practices may not be scientifically proven, they have cultural and historical significance in many societies. People find comfort and insights in these traditions, using them as tools for self-reflection and understanding their relationships with others. The blend of ancient wisdom and contemporary psychology has created a diverse landscape where individuals explore the dynamics of love through the lens of astrological and zodiac influences.